Life-Affirming Acts

Also in the CrossCurrents Series

Life-Affirming Acts

Education as Transformation in the Writing Classroom

Hector Julio Vila

Center for Educational Technology
Middlebury College
Middlebury, Vermont

New Perspectives in Rhetoric and Composition

CHARLES I. SCHUSTER, SERIES EDITOR

Boynton/Cook Publishers
HEINEMANN
Portsmouth, NH

Boynton/Cook Publishers, Inc.
A subsidiary of Reed Elsevier Inc.
361 Hanover Street
Portsmouth, NH 03801–3912
www.boyntoncook.com

Offices and agents throughout the world

The author and publisher wish to thank those who have generously given permission to reprint borrowed material:

Excerpt from *City on a Hill: Testing the American Dream at City College* by James Traub. Copyright © 1994 by James Traub. Reprinted by permission of Perseus Books Publishers, a member of Perseus Books, L.L.C.

Excerpts from *The Culture of Reading & the Teaching of English* by Kathleen McCormick. Published by St. Martin's Press, Inc., 1994. Reprinted by permission of the publisher.

Excerpt from "Ode to Failure" from *Collected Poems 1947–1980* by Allen Ginsberg. Copyright © 1984 by Allen Ginsberg. Reprinted by permission of HarperCollins, Inc.

Excerpts from *Teaching in America: The Slow Revolution* by Gerald Grant and Christine Murray, Cambridge, Mass.: Harvard University Press, Copyright © 1999 by the President and Fellows of Harvard College. Reprinted by permission of the publisher.

Library of Congress Cataloging-in-Publication Data
Vila, Hector J.
   Life-affirming acts : education as transformation in the writing classroom / Hector J. Vila.
     p. cm.
   Includes bibliographical references and index.
   ISBN 0-86709-560-1 (alk. paper)
    1. Socially handicapped—Education—New York (State)—New York—Language arts. 2. Language arts—New York (State)—New York. 3. English language—Composition and exercises—Study and teaching. I. Title.
LC4085.V55 2000
371.8—dc21   00-040385

Consulting Editor: Charles Schuster
Production: Sonja S. Chapman
Cover deisgn: Darci Mehall
Manufacturing: Louise Richardson

Printed in the United States of America on acid-free paper
04 03 02 01 00 DA 1 2 3 4 5

Contents

Prologue

I have always been intrigued by the specific moment when, as we sit waiting in the audience, the door to the stage opens and a performer steps into the light; or, to take the other perspective, the moment when a performer who waits in semidarkness sees the same door open, revealing the lights, the stage, and the audience ... I sense that stepping into the light is also a powerful metaphor for consciousness, for the birth of the knowing mind, for the simple and yet momentous coming of the sense of self into the world of the mental.
Antonio Damasio, *The Feeling of What Happens*

The truth is that if you want a well-governed state to be possible, you must find for your future rulers some way of life they like better than government; for only then will you have government by the truly rich, those, that is, whose riches consist not of gold, but of the true happiness of a good and rational life.
Plato, *"The Simile of the Cave"*

Anecdote of the Rope

A traffic light compels me into one of those arbitrary moments when motion ceases and we're able to ponder, so I begin to think that in failing—*by* failing, *then* reflecting—we learn; that failing nourishes the imagination by disclosing blind spots to us, areas we've missed or neglected, emphasizing the need for further study so we yearn for it. We grope on some level for failure because it gives sustenance.

I'm thinking this while watching a perfectly straight line of children walking slowly and bundled in wools, ski jackets, mittens and gloves, a rainbow of thinsulate and polartec to thwart Maine's piercing winter; they're pre-K, twelve to fifteen of them, their little left arms bent at the elbow, hands slightly raised, and each one singularly and uniformly clutching a long rope, on either end of which are a young blond in jeans and brown leather jacket and, holding the rear end of the rope, a more authoritative middle-aged woman, a writing pad in her free arm pressed against her chest.

I am fixated on the perfectly straight rope that doesn't give, not even a hint, when a child adjusts her weight or falters in step.

Ropes strangle failure, and forgiveness, is what I'm also thinking. Will we make it easy for these rope-kids to fail? Will we enable their failures by staging safe environments for their experimentation? What experiences are these children having as they grasp the rope, I wonder? What are they learning?

Teaching and learning are about seeing, *really seeing*, deeply, pene-tratingly, and in an environment that nurtures the audacity we require to experience and examine, fail and criticize, and then describe. *Life-Affirming Acts* is about this—about what I was seeing at the exact moment the children meandered across a Cumberland Farms parking lot and I waited for a green light.

Children look around in wonderment and amazement, their imag-inations overloading, wanting: Are they holding the rope or is the rope holding them? How much control will the children have over the rope? Who is guiding whom? What is the rope? Indoctrination? An object of *school as discipline*? The *status quo*?

Some undoubtedly say that this is an efficient way to walk pre-K children across a town enmeshed in midday urges and squabbles and responsibilities. When the children are on the rope, we keep them on track, we watch them, we make sure of their safety. But in our missions and obsessions, do we see these children, can we turn to them, or are they mere objects in our way, our heads pointing down the road, our feet on gas pedals, itching and eager to go?

This question is also a part of the scaffolding of *Life-Affirming Acts*. What, in fact, is at the end as well as the beginning of that rope? What is contained in that rope? Discipline? Indoctrination? Enlighten-ment? What? And how does that rope affect what we can—*or may*—become?

We live in an age of transition, a period of great potential brought about by ever-changing technologies that are revolutionizing our understanding of our world. We appear to have access to a greater abundance of information and knowledge and things, which gives us, perhaps, a false sense that we may be more capable, more powerful, in-dividually and collectively. We are literally and figuratively *wealthy*; we have the potential to achieve riches that are more about the true hap-piness of a good and rational life, as Plato says above. We say to our chil-dren, this future is theirs for the making. Do we ease their way, then? Will this help or hurt them?

But along with any renaissance comes evidence of disenfranchise-ment and marginalization. This *double bind*, the allure of great potential, on the one side, and the numbing affects of solipsism, mediocrity, and confusion on the other, are the poles characterizing our *fin de siecle renaissance*. If we look to our children, our students, those clutching the rope, we can see these extremes being played out. Places like Columbine will forever be signs of tragedy and fear—another twist of the same rope. Arguably, if nothing else, Columbine is a glaring example of how our children are crying out to us, assessing our every action, but we seem not to hear them—or will not hear them—until the darkest of tragedies begs our attention. In the final section of this book, *Complexion and Achievement*, a student writes, "Mostly at the high school level, students need to be accepted by their peers. This acceptance can give confidence and a sense of security in that there will always be someone there to comfort you whenever you may need it." Will there be?

A fundamental premise of *Life-Affirming Acts* is namely that we, as parents, teachers, and members of communities, are repressing—or rejecting—the language of our children and relying instead on staid and even oppressive methods of education, which do absolutely nothing to bring forth the spiritual and intellectual qualities of our students. We are therefore denying our students their desire, as well as their need, to venture out into the light—a prerequisite for realizing a "knowing mind," as neurologist Antonio R. Damasio tells us, above.

However, it is only by fulfilling their spiritual and intellectual potential that students will be able to create for themselves identities that are meaningful and moral and a good and rational life.

While prevalent throughout our educational system, nowhere is this more obvious than in our treatment of *minority* students who come to us from challenged socioeconomic communities. These students are destined for a *no-man's-land*, the world of remediation, a world marked by the vituperative politics of race and class.

Another important premise of *Life-Affirming Acts* is that we can turn this situation around, completely, and actualize our potential—if we work creatively and rely on *reflection-in-action* and *reflection-on-action*. This requires that we view ourselves, as well as our students, differently, first by putting into action the act of reflecting so as to determine what resides in our unconscious and thus facilitating honest expression in writing, then, second, by ensuring that we have the time to ponder our actions, our words, and how we got to them. This requires trust. And trust requires that we expose ourselves to our students in meaningful, honest ways so that they can bear witness to our trepidation and our fears, and can more fully grasp the journeys we have undertaken that led to their classrooms.

In essence, *Life-Affirming Acts* is about letting go of the rope—about how to begin to trust what students bring to our classrooms, and what teachers can produce when collaborating with students in nurturing, creative environments. *Life-Affirming Acts* is one description of a journey into trust, an imperfect journey that suggests how to loosen our holds on that rope and explains why we must.

Reading the Narrative

I did not want to produce a how to book about teaching composition: many already exist that have done a wonderful job of discussing this topic. I did, however, want to unveil the living, working classroom with all its imperfections—the messy art of teaching. Because if we want to speak of reform, the classroom needs to be totally exposed for what it is and for what it's not. I also want to show the origins of the work I demonstrate so that readers can more fully grasp my slant on issues, pedagogy, and critical theory, all of which are parts of the narrative. For this, I had to dig very deeply into the influences in my life that have made it possible for me to be "a teacher." *Life-Affirming Acts*, then, is structured as a narrative—a story of becoming.

The book is in three parts: *"Conflicts and Longings," "Hidden Voices,"* and *"Complexion and Achievement."* In keeping with postmodern sensibilities, *Life-Affirming Acts* can be read in different ways. The reader can move from cover to cover and experience the total narrative, or, once in each major part, a reader can replicate and use the subsections, or chapters, which describe the classroom, my reasons for the choices I've made, and the assignments I've given students. Taken as a whole, and in its narrative form, *Life-Affirming Acts* offers readers a semester's work graphically depicted.

In *"Conflicts and Longings,"* the chapters are *"Shedding Skins"* and *"Filling the Circle." "Shedding Skins"* is the narrative entry into an inner-city, remedial classroom as experienced by one shy, frightened and perhaps misunderstood student. It is this manner of storytelling that I perceive will show readers how an initial assignment on the first day of class takes shape; likewise, this first chapter exposes larger issues and themes relevant to the rest of the book. In essence, *"Shedding Skins"* begins to describe the highs and lows of the student-centered approach. *"Filling the Circle"* delves deeper into the remedial underworld, exposing current methods of working with remedial writing students. In keeping with the previous chapter, I demonstrate how I learned to turn this experience around by describing the extent of work needed to achieve trust and build confidence among students who have been beaten down. *"Shedding Skins"* and *"Filling the Circle,"* and *"Out of the Past"* thus offer readers a way to initiate a semester's work—a way to communicate with students that is perhaps more meaningful. *"Out of the Past"* is an example of a teacher's *reflection-in-action*, the source for the work in the previous sections.

Hidden Voices is the second part of the narrative. Chapter 4, *"What You Know, I Also Know,"* describes "a theory" or method for working with remedial students and literature by showing the two sides of remediation: one dictated by standardization, the other by imaginative, enabling work. In this more fully described student-centered classroom, students establish their context for reading and writing, reflect on their process, and begin to understand how they learn. In Chapter 5, *"Up From Mean Streets: Realism and Learning in a Renaissance Age,"* literature is introduced and highlighted against the recommendations of colleagues and the institution. The uses of literature for lifelong learning are illustrated through student experiences; likewise, comparisons between the remedial writing student and the mainstream student emerge, demonstrating that less is "wrong" with students that find themselves in this *no-man's-land* and more is "wrong" with higher education's perspective on students and education in general.

In the last part of the narrative, *"Complexion and Achievement,"* the issues, themes, and criticisms found earlier are synthesized by demonstrating how this approach has worked outside of remediation and in a post-Freshman Composition course, Introduction to Literature. Thus comparisons between remedial students and nonremedial students demonstrate that there is currently no difference between one world and the next given that higher education's perspective on students is relatively the same across the board. This final section is an argument as well as a method, for change—a prescription; it is also an invitation to readers to join in the journey.

Laced within these sections, within the entire narrative, are stories of my rather non-traditional education—the trials and tribulations that have gotten me to this point, and to this writing. These stories are vital, not because I speak about my history, but rather, because they remove release notions about *reflection-in-action* and *reflection-on-action* from theories and place them in the real world and in real practice.

Influences and Acknowledgments

A story such as this is long in the making. A long journey, by its nature, demands that the traveler acknowledge those, and there are many, who have had the greatest impact, the most profound influence on him or her because contrary to popular myth no journey, no book, is ever constructed in isolation; even when writing in solitude, visitations are constant, as William Blake has described.

My first and my most recondite teachers have been and continue to be my parents. Their journey has indeed been harrowing, though they've made mine easy. I can't begin to thank them, but I hope that in my own parenting I'm beginning to show the gratitude they deserve.

My sister, Susú, and my brother, César, have also traveled a major part of this journey. Undoubtedly, their stories differ from mine; however, since they too make up this small family circle so far away from our origins, their ideas, their laughter and humor, their insights, and above all, their tolerance of my inadequacies have affected my approach to the work before you.

I'm one of the lucky ones. I have had many excellent teachers. Sister Marie Francis began to change my life, slowly but surely. In a Catholic school environment I could not tolerate, she gave me the space and time—the safety—to begin to experiment with my voice. Sister Marie Francis took the time to notice me, and to urge me to grow.

I was also very fortunate to have attended Garden City High School, a public school on Long Island. I was too immature and young then to realize the lessons I learned there, but as I matured revisited them time and time again. I can still recall performing the courtroom scene of *To Kill a Mockingbird* in Stephen Castellano's class. Most of the time, I'm sure Mr. Castellano, who was also my homeroom teacher, didn't think I was listening, but I was. His humane treatment of literature, his love and passion for the work got to me and stayed with me ever since. Roger Goodwin was the first English teacher I had that, well, just let us "go." In my senior year, long before any notions of interdisciplinary work were in vogue, three of us wrote and produced two films for our class. Mr. Goodwin showed us how to reach toward our potential, he enabled us to be ourselves, to create our own constraints and contexts for learning.

At the University of South Florida, Professor Dan Wells "lived" literature, demonstrating to me that American literature and America itself are one in the same; the blood of America runs through our literature, and I experienced it in Professor Wells' class. It was a luxury. His thoroughness and professionalism, as well as his encouragement, provided a model that I've taken into every classroom. I've tried to honor literature in his way.

At New York University I entered a different domain, a high-stakes world—invigorating, challenging, and exciting. Anselm Haverkamp's gift for theory enabled me to fully comprehend the magnitude of philosophers' influences on our world. Frederick Karl, a truly gifted biographer, patiently allowed me to work in his domain, first with Conrad, then with Faulkner; his knowledge is vast and he shared it with me— I felt honored. John Maynard helped me to understand what a professor is, or should be, by simply and patiently urging me to talk about literature, that's all. But it was and still is Perry Meisel who most inspired me with his tenacity, his verve and his tremendous critical insight; his is truly a talented imagination. In my work on my dissertation on Henry James, Professor Meisel's criticism kept me going during difficult times.

A major part of this narrative occurs at Borough of Manhattan Community College, in New York City. I first thank my students, particularly Yesenia, who opened my eyes. These students gave their trust even when I didn't know what I was doing. That is a humbling—and frightening—experience. These students showed tremendous courage in the face of distressing conditions, both within their school and in their personal lives. The effects of racism and class structure—our collective societal indifference—are readily visible at BMCC; however, the magnitude of love and appreciation I received from these students, and their desire to learn, is something I've not experienced anywhere else.

Many colleagues in the English Department at BMCC tolerated my eccentricities. Phil Eggers, the department chair, simply let me go and supported the ideas of a nontenured, junior faculty member. He even participated in some of our experiments, a rare thing among department chairs. Jane Paznick, a friend, encouraged me and opened doors for my experimentation. My true mentor was Steve Cogan who educated me on German romanticism while challenging my every notion about teaching. Ruth Mischelof also encouraged me, pushing me and joining in my endeavors, testing out what I was trying to do. My office mate, Tricia Yi Chun Lin, always lent an honest ear and was a friend; we shared many laughs on the seventh floor—and we learned the ropes together. Nan Bauer Maglin literally changed my life by helping me professionally—a very selfless act. But it's been Nancy McClure who has been by my side at every turn, and to this very day. She read and commented on early versions of this manuscript when her time was limited; she advised me, challenged me, and pushed me; and she also paid me the best compliment anyone has ever given me: Nancy has worked through much of the material in this narrative, changing the lessons I describe in these pages to suite her needs. Nancy is an inspired teacher and gifted writer—a gem at BMCC. Her students and I are very fortunate; she gives us her all.

I spent eleven years as an adjunct at SUNY College at Purchase. Bill Baskin, dean and real friend, let me do what I wanted as long as the courses I taught had catchy titles! Bill made it possible for me to work through my dissertation: what I had to read became my courses. It is rare for a dean to step outside the norm, but Bill encouraged me to experiment, to strike out with new material and challenging perspectives.

I was also very fortunate to have worked with great, supportive people at William Paterson University. Ed Burns taught me the ropes, supported my work, and encouraged and guided me—a true friend.

Donna Perry, my office mate, is a giving and wonderful teacher who always took the time to ask me about my aspirations, then tried to help. Alice Deakins, a marvelous, giving teacher and a loving person, took the time to inquire about my work, adding welcome encouragement. Stanley Wertheim, a gentleman scholar in the full sense of the word, was always an interesting guide through the institution's quagmire, and also taught me about book collecting. Finally, Linda Hamalian, a giving and wonderful teacher who loves her students and her work, opened doors for me and enabled my interests; she remains a friend to this day. Anything Linda has done has turned to gold, this is her signature.

The seed for this book was planted during a Summer Invitational at the New York City Writing Project, Lehman College. Lynette Moorman and Ed Osterman have been friends, guides, and real teachers to me. Elaine Avedon has opened my eyes to very different and enabling approaches to the art of teaching. Ronni Tobman-Michelin, friend and co-teacher, has been "my partner in crime," if you will, working right along with me, experimenting and always looking for better ways to teach, better ways to work with writing.

Charles I. Schuster is my editor at Heinemann Boynton/Cook. His unfailing faith in my work sustained me throughout this long effort. Charles knows my writing better then I do at times, gently helping me to see and uncover the essence of my ideas. Charles is a genuine soul; his talents are boundless. And I've been blessed by his guidance. I would also like to thank Roberta Lew, at Heinemann, for guiding me through the intricacies and pitfalls of publishing. Lisa Luedeke and Eric Chalek, true professionals, are caring guides through the sometimes-daunting process of publication: they really take care of their authors. Anne Sauvé cleaned my "Spanishisms" from my English, tightened my prose, and made it fluid and suitable.

Ultimately, I have to thank my family. They've seen me through much during this writing, and put up with a lot, too. Carlos, the oldest, has literally been privy to my entire graduate education, my professional wanderings, and now this book; his patience and easy manner helped me in the most difficult of times, and I can't thank him enough for who he is—his easy manner and that smile like the sun. Chase, eager and energetic, tenacious and inquisitive, always lurking and asking about writing, literature, and film. He was my partner one summer: during the day I wrote a major portion of this manuscript and at night we watched films, discussing every angle. Chelsey, a dear soul and gifted child, a horse whisperer—and an amazingly talented writer has taught me how to appreciate and learn in very different ways—and through animals. Then there's Devon, who thinks himself a "scientific thinker." He brings joy and laughter to us all with his gift for language, his sparkly conversation, and his naturally tenacious character.

There's only been one person, however, for whom I write—my only audience, my soul mate, friend, and lover—my wife, Nina. She knows me better then I know myself; she nurtures all of us—she can't help that. Nina compels me to look at myself honestly. She patiently read the manuscript aloud, at every turn, critiqued, and urged. But most important, Nina has taken this giant leap with me because she trusts. She believes in me like no one else, so I hope I've done justice to her trust and belief.

Hector Julio Vila
Gorham, Maine, and
Middlebury, Vermont

Chapter One

Shedding Skins

The characters of nature are legible it is true; but they are not plain enough to enable those who run, to read them. We must make use of a cautious, I had almost said, a timorous method of proceeding. We must not attempt to fly, when we can scarcely pretend to creep.
Edmund Burke, *A Philosophical*
Enquiry into the Origin of
Our Ideas of the Sublime
and the Beautiful

There is one very beautiful proof, that people, when asked questions, if they are properly asked, say of themselves everything correctly; yet if there were not knowledge in them, and right reason, they would not be able to do this. You see, if you show someone a diagram or anything like that, he proves most clearly that this is true.
Plato, *Phaedo*

Her face is round and delicate, framed by thick, black hair. Her lips are full; her coal eyes sparkle: they say something. Sometimes, even on a sunny day, a blissful day, sad music reaches the heart and becomes overwhelming and reminds one of burdens. Her eyes remind me of this; they remind me of how deep melancholy can be when troubles are many.

She's involved in a pantomime, turning away when she knows I'm looking at her. Behind her ebony hair she's letting me know that getting to her will be hard. It's a resistance built on suffering, I'm sure.

Among the other women in the class she looks out of place, disoriented, unsure of what a student is, or how a student acts. Her actions say she believes there is *a student way*, so she looks for it, needing to add it to her *many ways*, her *many other roles*: *Here I am*, she's calling out. *I am here. I belong here.*

She is silent, fidgety, nervous.

She's a child wanting attention—yet in this adult world of the college classroom in an inner-city community college, she's competing for survival, she's struggling for her life. Her resistance is despair in disguise.

"Let's get to know each other," I say to my new writing class. "Let's get out a fresh piece of paper."

She labors with her hefty L. L. Bean backpack and pulls out a large, three-ringed binder, so big it makes her look even tinier than she is. Slowly, she pulls it open and dates her page in round, muscular lettering. These are her defining artifacts: *I go to school, to college,* these say. She gives importance to her public self, the sense of status or identity that only artifacts, when displayed, can produce. This is our culture's fixation, using artifacts to import significance, played out in her innocence, her naiveté, and her willingness to submit to *any means necessary* to survive—and *make it*, we like to say.

All of us, but teachers especially, have to pierce through this veneer of artificiality to get to the heart, where the voice resides, forgotten and deferred, yet still trying to emerge. Teachers struggle with L. L. Bean backpacks and other such things because students—all of us, really—have been silenced, accustomed to keeping our voices deep within recesses of our hearts, so we look to objects, or even to commercialized "messages," for our fantasies and respond only when spoken to, hopefully with the *right* answer.

Walter Ong (1982) suggests that, "literacy . . . is absolutely necessary for the development not only of science but also of history, philosophy, explicative understanding of literature and of any art, and indeed for the explanation of language (including oral speech) itself" (15). The survival of a culture is directly related to its promotion of orality which, in turn, produces "powerful and beautiful verbal performances of high artistic and human worth" (14).

No voice, no performance; no performance, no culture. Then there's only deprivation, anger, and ultimately death.

"Tell me something interesting about yourselves, introduce yourselves," I repeat to the class several times, and in different ways: *what makes you unique, tell me; what separates you from everyone else, come on; tell me something you're into that separates you from others; what ideas do you value, what ideas or goals do you have that you find most important and which then say something about you that's unique? Tell me.*

This is basic writing: cajoling, urging, pleading; scraping and scratching at tough skins to create avenues for voices to emerge and be heard. It's not neat; it can be messy; it doesn't always work out.

Come on! Yes! Speak!

William Faulkner said, in his soft, Southern voice, that all writers must be concerned with matters of the heart; these are the only things worth writing about. I imagine he said this because the heart is so difficult to get to know and understand; however, the journey there is exhilarating; the pain, drama, and passion enlightening. Faulkner always spoke fast, maybe because he needed to return to his writing, his heart.

The writing teacher's responsibility is to reach for the student's heart so that the student can behold, *yes, this is me, this is what I want to say*! The business of writing is the business of empowerment—and it's a difficult road. This is empowerment with discipline, with a price, unlike the empowerment presumed by the liberalist tendency to include virtually every current ethnic group's favorite theme or personage in one fourteen-week course. To tread the road I'm suggesting, the teacher must first be willing to search and reach her own heart and re-create it for the class, thus creating a text of herself for the class and others to interpret. "Reliving and reconceptualizing our experiences isn't just narcissistic," argues Ruth Vinz in *Composing a Teaching Life* (1996), "it's a way to effect new connections in experience and to see that what we set out to do has some underlying pattern, which sometimes needs to be challenged" (7). Simultaneously, then, for the teacher and the student, this is a spiritual act of awakening, a psychoanalytic act of self-examination—a shedding of skins; a creation of fields of knowledge to draw from, to write from. It is freeing, but as with any move toward freedom, the road is fraught with curves, bumps, and holes. Empowerment comes with a price.

Repeating my request to the class of remedial writers—*what makes you unique*—makes the students restless. Awkward glances and nervous smiles shoot about the room. The students are resisting. They are accustomed to resisting; it is built into education, promoting learning by rote and standardization, which is not the case here, so they are frightened.

Terms like *rote* and *standardization* can be numbing. We know this. If, as Stephen D. Brookfield tells us in *The Skillful Teacher* (1990), "teaching is experienced as deeply emotive and bafflingly chaotic" (1), and, likewise, "teaching is the educational equivalent of white-water rafting" (2), then we, too, understand that part of our mission is to convey this magnificence to our students. It is in this creative environment that imaginations flare. Rote and standardization kill this off, introducing negativity to an otherwise creative process. Students learn to reject everything and anything teachers try in a classroom.

Overcoming students' resistance to learning is not an easy matter. Brookfield is instructive here as well:

> Essentially, as most people realize, learning involves change. Since change is threatening, many people prefer to remain in situations that to outsiders seem wholly unsatisfactory, rather than to endure the psychological disruption represented by taking some kind of action. In all contexts of life we can see people for whom the threat of learning new behaviors or ideas is so unsettling that they remain in situations which will, in the long term, do them great harm. (147)

I knew that I was confronting this larger, more generalized—and dangerous—resistance. We were embarking on new terrain.

In some situations, though, tension is good. I want students to feel as if they are free-falling and there's no safety net. This is how to move toward the heart and through resistance. All varieties of subterfuge have kept students and teachers from their voices. We don't know who we are, or where we are going. Writing is a way out of this, an antidote to apathy. To students at Colgate University, on February 9, 1998, Kurt Vonnegut said acts of creation are "a way to make your soul grow" and a "spiritual adventure" (Park 1998). Writing and creating can bring this "spiritual adventure" back to the classroom but it's not easy, as I'm sure Vonnegut would agree.

A potential performance makes students nervous, bringing to the surface their collective thoughts about education's role in the subterfuge: *tell us **what** to know, **what** to do, **how** to be.* I've learned to interpret students' glances; this is what their nervous smiles say to me. They are not familiar with *let me find out for myself, guide me, but don't tell me; let me think, I'm entitled.*

"Mistah, watch u mean, *innerestin*? I donno *nothin innerestin* bout myself," a large black woman voices powerfully from the back of the classroom. She looks like she will swallow the desk beneath her. Her legs, her hands, her mass is overwhelming. She takes dominion of the room. *I am strong, black, and I'm beautiful,* she proudly speaks, demanding *notice me, here I am. A black princess.*

"Tell me something unique, what you like, what you're into. Or perhaps you have some interesting ambitions or goals. The only thing I ask is that you *don't* say, 'Hi, I'm a freshman, or sophomore, etc.' And please *don't* say, 'I attend Borough of Manhattan Community College.' These are interesting things, yes, but we want to learn what's unique about you. What got you here, to this place. Say something that shows the rest of us how different you *really* are."

"Oh, I see, yeah," the woman nods. Others nod too, smiling at each other, looking up at the lights, thinking; some turn immediately to their papers. The anxiety of performance has been supplanted by critical self-examination: *what's different about me? what should I say to show my uniqueness? what should I **not** say?*

They are editing and making choices about what they want to be today. They are writing—they are writing, beginning with what they know: themselves.

With her coal eyes sparkling, her round face beaming, the girl with the L. L. Bean backpack looks about the room, noticing the other women writing. She's still feeling out of place, wondering how she's going to belong, what she's going to use, what artifact to hide behind. She plays with the shoulder straps of her backpack. She then crosses her arms, shaking her head, *no,* and drops her gaze. Her long, black hair sweeps across her face like a curtain.

Fear, showing up as resistance, is a symptom of something larger, I think.

"Wait, wait, wait . . . Don't start yet," I say and grin diabolically. I want them to experience the play, the game, the fun in all of this. "Wait, there's one more thing before you start . . ."

"Ah, mistah, come on. I hates talkin bout myself." The princess in the back has somehow become the spokesperson of the class. We are in dialogue and the rest of the students are comfortable, nodding agreement. Sometimes this is how it happens: all speak through one: we're a culture accustomed to having our speech represented by hierarchies. Our media tells us this, too, so we have to work that much harder to become better readers of ourselves, the world around us, and of ourselves in the world around us.

"No, no, no. One more thing. It's simple. A couple of rules for this writing I want you to follow: first, I'm only giving you about three minutes to do this; second, I want you to make sure that each sentence you write is no longer than eight words. Eight words or less, that's all. Understand?"

"How we suppose to write—and count—together? It'll soun babyish, u know, we'll soun like little kids writin," says the princess spokesperson.

She is already talking about her writing. We have established the beginnings of a critical language, a way to dialogue about ourselves and our writing. It's a moment of enlightenment. These moments arrive unexpectedly, dropping like a bead of water that's been dangling from the edge of a leaf, and slowly, the weight becomes too much for the leaf and the drop releases, becoming something else. The climate changes: you must be ready for subtle changes. They happen all the time.

"No, don't worry. It'll be okay. You'll see," I urge. "All writers have limitations placed on them. Constraints enable the writer to produce.

You're just being introduced to one. You're working like writers now. You're going to sit in the writer's chair from now on. You *are* writers. Ready?"

"Yeah, wees ready," she says laconically—then laughs. "Can we start?"

"Everyone ready?"

Heads nod; swimmers take their mark; get set.

"Okay, begin."

*   *   *

Predictably, students look away when time is up and I ask, "Who wants to read first? Who will share her thoughts first? Come on, be brave, we'll all have to speak sooner or later. We'll always share in this class. Who'll speak first?"

Our private selves have been trained to be silent when faced by the overwhelming public. Schools have educated us to be silent, so when faced by the public domain, *the public sphere*, we cower, turn away, hide. We have turned Habermas' notion of a public sphere—the place to excite dialogue about differences—on its head and made it into a punishing, hostile environment. Schools have done their share in creating our disproportionate society.

As Victor Villanueva Jr. (1993) notes about his scholastic experiences in East Compton, California: "School becomes more a preparation for prison than for industry: doin' time" (5); and Mike Rose (1989) agrees: "Students will float to the mark you set. I and the others in the vocational classes were bobbing in pretty shallow water" (26). This is what students have learned quite thoroughly. But students momentarily forget all this while writing. In writing, they release prejudices and expose the mind thinking, creating a blueprint of the soul—where reflection can take place. Writing, or creating as Vonnegut calls it, is an antidote to the oppression we find in some educational institutions.

Students already sense this; it is obvious in their nervousness. Something from their unconscious may have surfaced and, they believe, ridicule might ensue: students anticipate public ridicule; accustomed to it, they look to conceal this brief exercise on the road to the heart with humor, or self-effacement, or even complicity with the ridicule they imagine yet to come. Ridicule is one of the fundamental characteristics of subterfuge.

I know they worry that the teacher will say in an all-too-familiar, caustic tone, *No. That's not right. Wrong.* I have had these teachers, too. It's the worry that the teacher is judge and executioner. *Tell me what you want*, students are accustomed to pleading. Students have learned that this is safer; they will not be *wrong* if they can imitate or parody the teacher. So students succumb to the teacher's—and the institution's—directions, methods, and even thoughts, believing they are involved in something creative, that their investigations are unique.

Students become silent once they learn that they are merely following orders; that their schooling is spent affirming the ambitions of authority; that school, and the institutions in our society, are concerned with power, and power, as Michel Foucault (1979) tells us, "has its principle not so much in a person as in a certain concerted distribution of bodies, surfaces, lights, gazes; in an arrangement whose internal mechanisms produce the relation in which individuals are caught up" (202).

We've been stifled and we don't know it: we don't know we have trouble seeing. It's part of an education strategy: suppress the imagination while simultaneously getting the student to think she is actively engaged in creation. Directions and impositions supplant creativity. Our system of education believes this is easier, *more cost-effective.*

"It occurred to me," notes Jonathan Kozol (1991), "that we had not been listening much to children in these recent years of 'summit conferences' on education, of severe reports and ominous prescriptions" (5).

So what are we left with?

Industrial Education

Mass training has standardized individuals both psychologically and in terms of individual qualifications and has produced the same phenomena as with other standardized masses: competition which creates the need for professional associations and leads to unemployment, over-production of qualified people by the education system, emigration, etc. (Gramsci 1988, 308)[1]

But writing—*creative writing*—challenges this stifling atmosphere. In *the act* of writing, the writer is compelled to experience herself as a part of the greater universe. The ego is released onto new terrain and thus awareness enters: the individual is present and active in her learning. Reflecting, the student notices interrelations between different forms of knowledge and begins to take command and makes choices. Learning is thus not imposed, but self-motivated and self-directed because *in the act* of writing the confines of the material world are released and the possibilities inherent in the imagination manifest themselves before the writer's very own eyes.

Creation *is* being—and you can't *be* unless you create. Writing, as an affirming, imaginative act, allows the writer to see her breath, feel her pulse, experience a connectedness to other things of which the self is only a cog. Anyone can do this.

Create an environment to release the student from her ego, and self-generated avenues for clear, honest perception will occur. Writing is releasing, which, in turn, enables the creation of something from what is sensed, from what we intuit, from what we know; it is slow and arduous, but gratifying—and achievable through constraints that enable inquiry.

As Judith and Geoffrey Summerfield (1986) suggest,

> To involve one's students in a short bout of unhappiness, frustration, and tension is an effective way of bringing them to appreciate some of the crucial differences between constraints that they feel to be legitimate and those that they feel to be illegitimate. They come to recognize legitimate constraints as fruitful, as yielding good results (like playing tennis with a net). They come to recognize illegitimate constraints as *merely* arbitrary, as inexplicable impositions, rules that are not susceptible of rationalizations that they can endorse. (7–8)

The composition classroom I am speaking about empowers the production of texts and promotes "an awareness not only of some of the crucial *features* of textuality but also of both the numerous options that at any moment the writer can see as available for choice, and of the constraints that inhere in any social act" (x). All writers are not identical.

I can say this about myself, yes, thinks the student hearing my initial prompt, the initial constraint. *Uhm, important, unique, what are these things?* she continues to wonder, searching beyond the physical restrictions represented by the classroom, editing herself and the world around her. *Eight words, no more. That's hard. How should I say this then?*

The teacher is saying, *Speak **your** thoughts.* Actually, I am *pleading.* I want them to *see* me struggle with *my work;* like theirs, it too comes from where the heart is. The teacher wants to expose this truth to create meaning: *this is important because it creates me . . . I will work with **your** work because it can define me . . . **this** is who I am!*

This way, and only this way, I believe, can both teachers and students come to realize themselves together: the teacher creates her vision of herself and the class, and the students, inhaling the teacher's creation, experience themselves in the interpretive act and so *recast* themselves in new lights which simultaneously *teach* the teacher.

So all of us must remember, and practice, that

> Who we are as teachers is constructed within a complex network of contradictory images from various sources . . . Every teacher needs to understand that the work of other teachers can become part of the dialectic on teaching, but it cannot essentialize each individual teacher's work. (Vinz 1996, 5–9)

No exit from performance—for anyone! And no exit from assessment—the student's of us, the teachers—or from perhaps the most poignant gauge—the character, stability, and health of our culture!

The subterfuge usually existing between teacher and students in the writing class is a symptom of an atmosphere mired in rules, regulations, and restrictions associated with repressive forms of composition loosely labeled *standards*, and is the sign of an unhealthy culture. It is removed and supplanted by the realization—the epiphany—that *there are only learners*. No other distinction is necessary. This occurs by writing *and* talking *and* reading.

*   *   *

"Be brave. Who'll be the first brave soul?" I urge the students in my class, again and again, then look languidly, beckoning the princess to speak once more, this time for all of us. My eyes tell her *I need you. Read for me*, they plead; they say, *teach, teach all of us through you*. I bow my head ever so slightly, like a genuflection I hope only she can understand. *Please*.

"Oh, all right," she speaks out, taking hold of the public sphere. Everyone, momentarily relieved, turns to her.

"Hi. I'm Kisha . . ."

Then she looks up from her paper to all of us, saying, "U all know dat . . ."

"My life is my son, Jason. He like his fatha, strong willed. I'm always in his school pushin his teachers. He ain't gonna end up in no jail. Not dead eitha. So I'm gettin an education to move away. Maybe go back souff to my family. But I needs noise. It's too quiet in the country. I love the noise of the streets."

Kisha opens doors for us to walk through. She is making my task easier. *Thank you*, I genuflect again. The class is immediately engaged; feeling safe, they gravitate to Kisha, princess *and* public persona. A writer. Kisha has begun to narrate the story of the class—and it begins with her.

"How old is your son?" someone asks, wanting more.

"Eight."

"Mines' five."

"I have four," says another woman.

"Four! I don't want no kids. No sir. They'd drive me crazy," intervenes someone else. "Besides mens don't wanna help. They do *it* an leave."

Laughter. "Ah-hum, dat's right. Yeah, no good," travels the classroom.

Everyone is speaking at once. The class—the silence—is overwhelmed by the wave of public speech. The spell has been broken. Writing and performance are linked. Orality is present. It's now safer.

We're in a different room, a less fragile room. Egos have been released. The first skin has been shed.

Someone else volunteers to speak. "I'll go. I'll do mines . . ."

Then another, and another . . . "Me. Let me go. I wanna try . . ."

We hear about wanting to be a teacher; African village life and traditions; "I wanna serve my community"; a hysterectomy: "they always do dat to us on welfare. We don need it, but they do it"; wanting a home, a family, a good career; riches; God; "I want a Ph.D., eventually," says one woman; a *good* man, wants another.

It's music: a symphony of singular voices uniting in an open public space they define. They draw me in. We are together. We're writing in key. It's intoxicating, they're intoxicating, alive, celebrating each other and their writings.

"I wanna do what I want. Nobody tellin me nothin"; "I want my sistah's killer to be caught. I want him killed". Another student says she wants to work to help people "see how alike we are. We want the same things. We can get along"; "I wanna be a lawyer and help people. Some people have no representation"; "to change my life" comes up a lot, as do insurmountable obstacles of daily lives; *Reality*, they say.

Students are a microcosm of the world outside the classroom. They bring it in; they want to *speak it, define it, characterize it*—then define themselves in it. This is their canvas; they've established the world they want to re-order by writing.

I see myself transforming and becoming inextricably linked to these students' voices as I try to create the atmosphere for their narratives to come to fruition. I see myself, the *teacher* who, in trying to demonstrate writing, will have to allow his vulnerabilities to emerge, exposing himself to the students' imaginings. And I see myself, the *student* who, having learned in other ways and in other, more *traditional* places, is seeking the guidance of not-so-traditional teachers.

I see myself as *their student*, which I find is the only way to be a teacher, and the only way to assess what we are collectively trying to create: identities compliant to our intimate visions of the contexts of our worlds.

"They thinks jus because we women and we black, and there ain't no man around, we stupid. They treat us like shit, like we don even exist. We have no feelings. We can't think," says another student, abruptly and without prompting, but evidently feeling the comfort of the enabling atmosphere of the classroom.

This darkens the atmosphere. Some cast their eyes downward.

The melancholy hanging in the air brings me back to her coal-black, downcast eyes again, her black hair that she uses to hide behind. She becomes the foreground. I realize that throughout this exercise, as Kisha spoke, as everyone else chimed in, from the corner of my eye, in

the center of my mind, her delicate, round face—her demeanor—
struck a persistent tone. Like a siren's song, it was a voice consonant
with my imagination: *Where is she? Why is she not with us? Why am I not
connecting with her? What does she need?*

"What's your name?"

The class is silent, watching. It's too obvious, her place outside the
euphoria, the arena of public speech, the writing.

"Yesenia."

"What a beautiful name. Where are you from?"

In a mixture of accents, a dialect specific to New York, "Nuevayork," she says, "Portorico," then returns to her silence, looking away.

Questions and answers. Yesenia will tell her story one line at a time,
one word at a time. She takes control of the class differently than Kisha
had earlier: The two extremes, the two powers: overwhelming presence
and diminutive innocence, yet both coming from where fear dwells.

"What have you written?"

"Notin."

"Nothing? You've written nothing about yourself?"

"No."

"Why?"

"I *hh*ave notin interestin. I don know," she shrugs. "Notin," she says
smiling and blushing.

"You're unique. I *know* you're interesting. Just in your responses.
Right now. What you're saying *is* interesting."

"I'm not interestin, *dat's* interestin?"

"That's not what you're saying. You're saying something else."

Yesenia sits up. Fidgets. Crosses and uncrosses her legs. Looks at
the round lettering of her date, then the blank page. "Whatta I mean
then?"

"Yesenia," I say and move closer to her, face-to-face, eyes-to-eyes.
I want her to transcend her fears; I want her to begin the journey into
self-fulfillment, as the others have done. I want her to realize that this
classroom is like a giant safety net where she can take chances and not
be condemned.

Her eyes are two round caverns, deep and solemn. This is where
fear lurks. "Yesenia. Don't be afraid. Did I say anything that would
make anyone in this class feel bad about themselves?"

"No."

"Did you like what you heard here today, what the others said?"

"Uh-huh. It's nice. It was good."

"At first it was difficult for everyone, like it is for you. But they did
it; it wasn't too painful, not too much—at least I think it wasn't."

Several in the class help me out, help out Yesenia. "Yeah, he all
right, Jesenia. He all right. U see. Yeah."

"I don wanna talk about myself. I don like to espeak about my private life."

"You don't have to say anything about your private life. Tell us something you value, something you *can* speak about."

"My daughter. She's beautiful. Look," she says reaching into her L. L. Bean backpack and pulling out a key chain with a picture of her daughter. A small, round-eyed little Yesenia looks out at me.

"She's beautiful. She looks just like her mother. I'm sure you're a wonderful mother and you want the best for her."

"Jes. She's two. Taisha keep me real beezee."

"Beautiful. See. You did it. You've told us something very significant and interesting about yourself. Wonderful."

The class applauds: *See.*

"But I ain gonna talk about myself. Joose ain gonna *hh*ave us always do dis, no? I'll die if joo do . . . I'll fail . . ."

We perceive fear and failure and vulnerabilities to be obstinate intruders to our creative inclinations, to our need to communicate and share—and imagine; we perceive them as festering, unwelcome partners in a classroom—or anywhere else for that matter. Obstacles. Seldom do we experience fear, failure, and vulnerabilities as motivations for creativity. We want to display security. It's the American way, security. We spend a lot of time talking about it.

I am left to wonder where Yesenia has learned to see failure as something to be avoided to such an extreme that she cannot see that she is actually voicing a desire to participate, though she doesn't know quite how to go about it. This fear of failure is paralyzing, blinding—so you can't write. You need to see to write, and vice versa.

In her reluctance, in her search for *a student way*, Yesenia is saying, *make it safe for me to try, and if I do, will I be all right, will you take care of me and no one laugh*? She doesn't see herself as having ever experienced success, though she is a proud mother. Her pride begins and ends with birthing and the beauty of *mi bebé*, not with what comes after. The affirming rewards of motherhood elude her. *Motherhood* is a metaphor for struggle and loneliness, the signs of survival; existing is surviving. In Spanish it's called *sobrevivir*. It's meager.

Yesenia *is* creation squandered, imagination lulled to sleep. This is the perspective I am compelled to take. We are born with capabilities, a desire to inquire and to learn, and imagination; however, sitting before me in this dull, gray room with plastic desks and barely a view of Greenwich Street bustling with financiers at lunch time is a portrait of despair; Yesenia is *etherized*, T. S. Eliot would say. She is a bird with clipped wings looking for a nest from which to begin to fly anew, except that the nests have been taken away. She has been done in. Crippled and handicapped by circumstances—and institutions—Yesenia can only see herself as an advertisement for the college student, a proposition manifested in the language of her large binder and L. L. Bean backpack. Whatever was *planted* in Yesenia is lost, rooted out.

She is frightened that she might be a forgery. Yesenia, and many like her, must reenter herself in order to begin to become familiar with an imagination polluted by advertisements, mass-media junk, and circumstances. Lost somewhere in her adolescence is her willingness to leap creatively into the unknown. She prefers the familiarity of being told what to do, and how to do it.

And she is only twenty-one, a mother who will pass these facts onto her daughter, Taisha. It is a cycle of despair and fear—and it is costly, literally and figuratively.

There has to be a better way, a less frustrating way, a less damaging way.

This was the first day of class; it wasn't neat. It got messy at times and I didn't know what would work; neither did the students. We were moving ahead cautiously. We were not yet flying; rather, we were proceeding in a timorous fashion, scarcely creeping. But we finally managed to place our desks in a circle.

Note

1. There's plenty of evidence to support Gramsci's statement. We need not look further than, say, education's overproduction of Ph.D.s: we have too little jobs for the slew of Ph.D.s granted, not only feeding unemployment among higher education, but fueling the cruel adjunct system; in business, NAFTA has had much to do with moving "labor" offshore; and, in the growing world of technology, we did not forecast the needs for systems engineers and programmers, so here, too, we're looking offshore. The technology world is being pushed by "big money made quickly," rather than by insightful management and examination of what we've achieved and what this might mean for our future. The ironic tragedy is that we don't have enough teachers in grades K–12; we don't have adequate space to house a growing, and very different, student population; and we're slow, even reluctant to make the technology expenditures to assist students to be avid, creative contributors in the "information age." We're overproducing and overqualified, so we're standardizing along class lines. We experience this as truth, a given.

Chapter Two

Filling the Circle

On the board she had written two columns of phrases. The first, headed "Student Problems," consisted of the following:

> *too much work*
> *too difficult life*
> *small disasters*

The second, labeled "Problems with Student Work," included:

> *late/absence*
> *inc. or sloppy work*
> *disaster of journals*

> *Drabik called me after class one day and asked how I thought things were going. When I had told her how much trouble the students were having with Macbeth, she sighed and said, "It's better I do not know this."*

James Traub, *City on a Hill*

As one possible solution to this apparent absence of "critical reading," students need to learn to locate the texts they read, as well as themselves as reading subjects, within larger social contexts; in short, they need to be able to inquire into and understand the interconnectedness of social conditions and the reading and writing practices of a culture.

Kathleen McCormick,
*The Culture of Reading and
the Teaching of English*

On the second day of class, the students' faces are more defined, more familiar, as probably the teacher's is to the students.

The room is clearer, brighter, and subtleties begin to emerge: someone sits, slouched, notebook opened, indifferently doodling; someone else sits erect, watching and waiting; students' fingers are tipped by black fingernails, red fingernails, glistening, designer nails; heavy, half-moon gold earrings hang from someone's ears; many different sized and shaped earrings dot another's earlobe; hair, lots of it, in waves and colors and curls, short and long, round and angular—jheri curls, pomade, pergamont grease—crown the profusion of faces.

Style is everywhere, forceful and powerful; rhythmically, boldly, and harmoniously, students fill the classroom: it expands.

But the desks are not in a circle. The janitor has seen to that, breaking up the circle of the first day into rows for the second. He's been told students sit in rows, in customary ways. There is no circle to be filled yet. This symphony of style has to be recomposed and redirected.

On the second day of class the teacher must already have made a decision: whether to enter among these faces, or not; whether to stand in front of the class, or amongst the students, within the circle. This makes all the difference in the world. Customary ways need disrupting.

Let's place the desks in a circle.

Loud scratching, ruckus, shuffling, and we all face each other now: new visions and challenged perspectives. The circle suggests that we're going to do things a little differently; we're going to face things, each other and ourselves.

If McCormick (1994) is even remotely correct, that students "need to be able to inquire into and understand the interconnectedness of social conditions and the reading and writing practices of a culture" (7), then the teacher must provide the creative outlets for students to express *their* understanding of the culture and, thus, view themselves as subjects. In other words, students express to the teacher what they think she represents; they teach themselves, using the teacher as vessel or sounding board.

To establish these complex methods of working in a writing class, teachers must synthesize different writing-to-learn activities to enable writers to reach *into* themselves and their readings of their elaborate worlds. Central to this process is the use of a journal—a place where students can "play." Journals are sacred terrain where students feel less constricted and can generate great ideas for further inquiry and development, probably because they are not worried about audience.

Although plenty of literature exists about the efficacy of journals, I find Peter Elbow and Jennifer Clarke's chapter, "Desert Island

Discourse: The Benefits of Ignoring Audience," from *The Journal Book* (Fulweiler 1987), still very instructive:

> The value of learning to ignore audience while writing, then, is the value of learning to cultivate the private dimension: the value of writing to make meaning to oneself, not just to others. This involves learning to free oneself (to some extent, anyway) from the enormous power exerted by society and others: to unhook oneself from external prompts and social stimuli . . . Though writing is deeply social and though we must also practice enhancing the social dimension of writing, writing is also the mode of discourse best suited to helping us develop the reflective and private dimension of our mental lives. (32)

Thus, we can see quite clearly how a Chinese student named Pamela, who is in remedial writing at Borough of Manhattan Community College, is able to establish an understanding of herself *through* writing, beginning with a freewriting exercise done in a journal, then moving through a series of prompts, and, finally, to her essay. This working pattern—freewriting to focused freewriting or prompting to drafts—is a design I usually establish at the beginning of the term; customarily, this routine will last throughout an entire semester. And as we'll see later, it's also a worthwhile method for introducing literature into a writing class.

Pamela writes in her journal:

> When I first came here two years ago, my parents grabbed me by the hand and took me to my first English school. They pushed me almost all the way to the school because I didn't want to study English. They finally got me there and they paid for all the first courses. Wow, when I see my parents, I just say, "God Bless You!" because they sure woke me up about this important language of the world.

In this personal—and *free*—reflection we can begin to understand Pamela's world, new and perhaps forbidding. What can we do with this reflection, though? What can we offer to James Traub and his teacher, Professor Drabik, from the epigraph above, as a methodology that might be more inclusive of students?

I offer students different ways of reentering their freewriting. I like to establish a methodology whereby throughout a term we systematically revisit what we've already written, then reflect and revise. This way, revision is never a point of struggle, especially among beginning writers, who have so many contentions. Rather, it is experienced as a fluid and dynamic part of an entire process, a journey or inquiry into one's self. This process is then refrabricated as an illustration of one's self on paper—and for an audience.

One way to begin is to ask students to revisit their work and write a letter to themselves about the issues they surmise are most relevant, or that "stick out" most glaringly.

> Dear Me,
>   I didn't take any English courses in College before. In high school, the teachers only taught me the simple grammar and writing of English. They didn't need me to write a whole essay. Therefore, my writing skill is really poor. If I have to write an essay at least 500 words, I think I can only write about 300 words and use so much time. Based on what I know so far, maybe I get a lot of mistakes. I think I should concentrate on the content of an essay.

In her letter to herself, Pamela gives us further insights into her world. As McCormick puts it, Pamela is indeed learning "to locate" herself "as the reading subject"; once she's introduced to a text, she'll read it, and herself, "within a larger social context." Pamela is beginning to learn how to negotiate these sometimes elusive avenues. For instance, she describes her earlier, high school experience as concentrated on grammar and realizes that this has not been enough. She understands that her high school experience didn't prepare her for "the essay." Having "failed" the WAT, the CUNY (City University of New York) Writing Assessment Test, which landed her in Remedial Writing, Pamela now understands that there's an issue of time involved; that her expertise is insufficient to meet the demands of time, grammar and syntax, and well-developed content. But, interestingly, she decides that she "should concentrate on the content of an essay"—admirable resolve.

A simple exercise like this would give Professor Drabik an understanding of "Student Problems," a realization as to why these students may be experiencing "too much work," a "too difficult life," and "small disasters." Teachers' lists of students' problems—"late/absence," "inc. or sloppy work," "disaster of journals"—solve nothing in the remedial world. Rather than not knowing what students don't understand about *Macbeth*, is it not wiser for the good professor first to understand where and if *Macbeth* exists in their world? This makes for a much more interesting class for teachers and students.

This, too, causes a reversal of roles in the classroom, which can be frightening because the teacher relinquishes her traditional role so that students can determine their own interconnectedness with the culture's modes of conditioning citizenry.

Following the "Dear Me" letter, I give students a series of prompts, focusing their attention on issues I want them to spend some time with during a three-week period. Mind you, I've not examined their journals yet, a process that I do routinely every three weeks, so I don't know anything about what Pamela's written. I give them approximately seven to eight minutes between prompts, the first one of which is Identity. "Absolutely sameness," writes Pamela. "Exact likeness—who she is." For Custom/Tradition, she writes: "Usual and general accepted behavior among members of a social group." And, finally, Self-Reliance she defines as, "Showing confidence in one's own powers, judgments."

I use these prompts to focus the student's attention on what we're about to read, as well as to connect them to what they have been writing, freely and openly, in their journals. I introduce Gwendolyn Brooks' "a song in the front yard," which we read through entirely, one time. The reading is followed by a reflective writing.

In Pamela's entry we can see where her worlds come together:

> I don't really understand what the poem is about. Maybe, it is about growing up to be a bad woman. The poem said I've stayed in the front yard all my life where it's rough and unattended and hungry weeds grow. A girl gets sick of a rose. I think a girl was born in a dirty and poor place. She didn't have a good time. She was sick of that place. She wanted to go in the backyard. To where the charity children play. She wanted to get some fun and leave the poor place. She wanted to change her life from poor to rich. But, on the other hand, she was fine to be a bad woman. She didn't feel anything bad for wearing the brave stockings of night-black lace and strutting down the streets with paint on her face. She couldn't go back. She had to live with bad things.

As Plato contends, students already know, they merely have to be taken to recollection. In other words, the means have to be provided for students to spend time inquiring about what they already know and understand. This is the work of perspective, the achieving of it, the sculpting of it, the arduous pleasure arising from phrases never before experienced stating something differently, honestly. It's colorful and it's exciting. Traub's (1994) Professor Drabik has turned away from this, turned her back on her students. She's in darkness because she is relying on a lost antidialogical and noncommunicative model of education that is aggressively opposed to real interventions and to historical awareness itself. "It's better I do not know this" (8–9), she says laconically, decontextualizing her lessons and, most important and tragical, her students as well. In Traub's classroom description, promoting silence represses intimacy's importance to the education process, doing irrevocable damage.

A writing class, a literature/writing class—*any* class, actually—is an investigation into ways of negotiating the culture's techniques for creating subjects. Let me repeat that in another way: the classroom's place in our culture is to excite inquiry into historical awareness and real, authentic thinking. But this can be threatening, especially since accepted cultural constructions come into question in the process. Although in Pamela's case, we can argue that her reading of Brooks' poem is a literal one, once we compare her reading with her journal's free-writing we can't fail to understand that her ethnicity is a part of her response, from the opening "I don't really understand," which notes a degree of apprehension, to "she is sick of that place," showing an understanding of the character's disgruntled outlook and, finally, to "she wanted to change her life from poor to rich," a recognition, that "change" can sometimes improve one's condition. Was Pamela thinking of her own condition?

It's not that Pamela doesn't understand Brooks; it's that Brooks is confusing because she's presenting a model of the world that, despite some recognizable descriptions, is disconcerting when taken as a whole, especially for someone who is of Chinese origin with strong family and national alliances.

And since Brooks is questioning such concepts as Identity, Customs and Traditions, as well as Self-Reliance—a fact not lost during our class discussion of the poem—writing begins to be understood as an aggressive act, a political act—even, perhaps, a liberating act. The self expresses itself against all odds and all cultural conditioning; it is an existential expression affirming one's role, function, and potential in a society. Writing, viewed this way, is a tool for achieving an identity through perspective. It can metamorphose a culture, one individual at a time.

In her final essay, and after examining everything we had written to date, we can see how Pamela is working very hard to contextualize her reading and writing experiences:

> For many foreigners, they have a strong feeling of nationalism for their own countries. This doesn't mean that they dislike America, but they are proud of their countries more than being proud to be Americans. They don't forget their countries and cultures. They always remember what nation they belong to. Before I came to study in the United States, my father told me that I had to always be proud of my country and be Chinese. I only came to the United States to get an education. I am not going to be an American and stay forever.
>
> There are many different meanings to "Identity." In the poem, "a song in the front yard," the girl is not happy with who she is. She wants to change, so she sees herself being like those women who "strut down the streets with paint" on their faces. She thinks it's okay to be this way. But she's going against the wishes of her mother.
>
> I, on the other hand, have a strong feeling of nationalism from my father. Before I left to come to the United States, my father gave me his credit card and told me to go wherever I wanted. So with my

friends, we went to see the Great Wall of China and a lot of temples. The trip was expensive, but I wanted to be careful with my father's money because he was so generous. We went to China's historical sites because we have a lot of pride in who we are. My "identity" is Chinese, but I can understand why the girl in the poem may want something different. We all have these feelings. This is why when I'm studying in the United States, I'll experience different things I'll be able to take back home with me.

The models oppressing students, silencing their voices, are delivered *through* the teacher. It is one of the primary functions of much mainstream education: to socialize through models that the dominant class upholds and glorifies, votes for, and pays for—then demands. The demands come in the form of discipline, a process accommodating modes of behavior that maintain the status quo but don't solve problems.

A teacher entrenched in the front of the class—the idol of status quo discipline and socialization—imposes her view of the culture onto students and affirms already accepted cultural constructions, as Drabik does, then suffers the consequences because she fails to see herself as promoting and simultaneously existing in the same repressive model as her students: *please don't tell me what I don't want to know; that they don't understand what I understand; that I don't know how to reach them, though they are reaching me since I already* **do know**—*I can see—that they are having problems*. This is the teacher in denial of her sensibilities and afraid of changing. Students are foreign to this teacher; she wants them to be like her—and they can't be, or they refuse to be. So she blames them.

We do this quite well in education; in fact, we promote this methodology.

Is there another possible way of doing this? students call out.

What would Emerson say, I wonder?

In this distribution of functions the scholar is the delegated intellect. In the right state he is *Man Thinking*. In the degenerate state, when the victim of society, he tends to become a mere thinker, or still worse, the parrot of other men's thinking.

In this view of him, as Man Thinking, the theory of his office is contained. Him Nature solicits with all her placid, all her monitory pictures; him the past instructs; him the future invites. Is not indeed every man a student, and do not all things exist for the student's behoof? (Emerson 1960, 65)

Drabik will never know what her students know if she doesn't change; she will never become realized *through* her students *and* her teaching if she doesn't learn to enter her students' lives and thus enable them to recontextualize her curriculum. Drabik does not see herself as a student, and she's not willing to do so; instead, she thinks and acts like a traffic cop, a marshal, a barometer of what is happening to her ancient, staid ways: they are killing off students, and Drabik herself. Dialogue is not evident in this classroom. She is involved in a repudiation of Nature and, tragically, she doesn't realize it.

Teachers become fully realized in the act of teaching. Students realize themselves, too, learning not only about themselves, but also and perhaps more important, about how they learn. Teaching is an all-encompassing art tied to experience: we're all teachers, whether we're conscious of this or not. It's the most natural, affirming act we perform daily.

As Pamela writes further on in her essay, "Children can only follow what parents tell them. In our society, few people have power, but people want to show confidence. They get their own opinions and beliefs. They want to show that they have their own powers."

Emerson tells us that "Life lies behind us as the quarry from whence we get tiles and copestones for the masonry of today. This is the way to learn grammar" (71). I would argue that Pamela is on her way to Emerson's realization; and that she's also learning that this process involves "reflection-on-action" and "reflection-in-action." Thus, reflection, says Vinz (1996), "is both a response to puzzlements and an act of creation . . . [it] urges episodic, spontaneous, and digressive thoughts and often triggers various responses to particular situations, actions, or ideas" (106–108). It is creation unrestrained, or if mitigated, it is done so by the individual's command. This too is quite natural, though we've gone to great lengths to suppress it.

"Writing," says Roland Barthes (1977), "begins at the point where speech becomes *impossible* (a word that can be understood in the sense it has when applied to a child)"; so "it is not knowledge which is exposed, it is the subject (who exposes himself to all sorts of painful adventures)" (190–194). This is transformative because students give their voices to the teacher, to the class; they speak to the teacher through nuance, innuendo, and subtlety—and the teacher speaks back, after reflection, *to invite reflection*:

> . . . for the teacher, the student audience is still the exemplary Other in that it *has an air* of not speaking—and thus, from the bosom of its apparent flatness, speaks in you so much the louder: its implicit speech, which is mine, touches me all the more in that I am not encumbered by its discourse. (195–196)

A teacher must reside within her audience so as to listen and hear the voices, the students' and hers. A teacher cannot learn and grow if she refuses to be among her students, to fill the circle of desks with their knowledge, and complement it with her own. This is growth; this is also enlightened thinking that has existed from Socrates to Paulo

Freire. James Traub's two examples in the epigraph, and the subsequent failure of his *City on a Hill* (1994), a hostile critique of New York's City College's attempts to deal with remediation and the changing complexion of its student body, realities which Traub abhors, demonstrate a blindness motivated by the need to follow models of education that assume that we exist in a homogeneous culture, something Traub obviously pines for, not the culture of the students we have today, whether these be African Americans, Hispanics, Eastern Europeans, Asians, or what we think are middle-class, traditional American students—the MTV/Generation X crowd.[1]

The frustration Traub chronicles in *City on a Hill* is predicated by the culture's vertical value system that students are taught to embrace and that is made poignantly evident by the metaphor they visit daily—the rows of desks; in fact, Traub advocates a return to this "old world": climb the hierarchy or else; the bottom rung is the lowest and the most painful. Traub's *exposé* pines for bygone days in education where all the students were homogeneous and the teacher merely lectured while the students did exactly as they were told. Perhaps this picture of the world never existed; certainly, though, during a time when global communications were not shrinking the world and disparate cultures were not sitting side by side in classrooms, education was much simpler to deliver. But since our illusions about what the world and education might have been like when "things were simpler" is being challenged, and in some quarters actually being changed, we've become punitive and aggressive in our confusions.

> While the rightist sectarian, closing himself in "his" truth, does no more than fulfill his natural role, the leftist who becomes sectarian and rigid negates his very nature. Each, however, as he revolves about "his" truth, feels threatened if that truth is questioned. (Freire 1972, 23)

Thus, we suffer from being accomplices in our own silencing, allowing for no movement at all, maintaining the firmly placed socioeconomic binds of a culture. *Gridlock*. Imagine a vice grip on the imagination's potential. *City on a Hill* is not "testing" whether the American Dream exists at City College; it is, rather, a relentless examination of how idiomatic, punitive, and therefore *un*-educating higher education can be. It is a blueprint for how to actually *close the American mind*. *City on a Hill* suggests that it's the *old* way, or *no* way; the culture depends on it. We believe it to be economically viable, ironically since we are stupefying potential.

How can a culture achieve excellence or health if institutions are involved in maintaining the status quo? Our creativity is sapped; unable to budge, and angered that the old methods don't seem to work anymore, frustration sets in and we castigate.

> The European immigrants didn't need City [College] anymore; it was the black and Puerto Rican citizens of Harlem, the people who for years had looked up the hill at the remote campus, who needed it now . . . City College's glorious past remains legible, if sometimes only faintly, beneath the accretions of its contemporary life . . . Hidden from view, and extending far downward, is City's vast remedial under-world . . . One large body of students stretches below the core; another stretches above. It's only a slight exaggeration to say that City is really two colleges, a liberal arts/professional institution and a remedial/open admissions one. (Traub 1994, 11–13)

The deluded dependency on ambiguous hierarchies—"the black and Puerto Rican citizens of Harlem, the people who for years had looked up the hill at the remote campus"—coupled with the anger permeating unmet needs—"City College's glorious past remains legible, if sometimes only faintly, beneath the accretions of its contemporary life"—compels City College not to create positive solutions, but rather, to impose oppressive and bleak obstacles to human and cultural growth: "One large body of students stretches below the core; another stretches above."

Thus society has *re*-created the stringent model of a culture forcefully bent on a vertical, hierarchical view of itself, where some of its citizens must reside in sub-basements, dark and abysmal, where rage builds "far downward, in City's remedial underworld" of apathy, despair, and malaise.

It's no wonder that teachers find no recourse but to demean students, become negative, and eventually *burn out*, as we like to say, or leave the profession prematurely. No one learns, so things stay as they are. In frustration, teachers replicate the means of an oppressive education model. But we're still left wondering: Are we encouraged, by the system, to know and respond to the concrete realities of this world? Are we equipped? Are the concrete realities of this world kept submerged because these require so much critical self-awareness?

What is obviously not submerged is a willful racist agenda condemning Puerto Ricans and other people of color for not embracing the failing nineteenth-century European models of discipline and education. We are, in fact, blaming the new wave of immigrants in our schools—Central and South Americans, Asians, Africans—for challenging our homogeneous appearance, our homogeneous approaches to our cultural problems.

As Jonathan Kozol notes in *Amazing Grace* (1995) when he is taken by Gizelle Luke, Covenant House's program director, to a location "a couple of blocks from Shakespeare Avenue to an overpass that crosses the expressway, which . . . leads to the suburbs and the interstate, I-95," and where "the pictures of flowers, window shades and curtains and interiors of pretty-looking rooms . . . have been painted on these buildings on the sides that face the highway":

> The city had these murals painted on the walls . . . not for the people in the neighborhood—because they're facing the wrong way—but for tourists and commuters. "The idea is that they mustn't be upset by knowing too much about the population here. It isn't enough that these people are sequestered. It's also important that their presence be disguised or 'sweetened.' The city did not repair the buildings so that kids who live around here could, in fact, *have* pretty rooms like those. Instead, they *painted* pretty rooms on the facades. It's an illusion." (30–31)

City on a Hill is another "*painted* pretty room" for us who live on the suburb side to feel affirmed. The problem is, of course, that Traub is in fact a tourist, a commuter, as we may all be, conjuring hymns of loss for institutions that have always been questionable and are now utilized to marginalize all citizens. This is symptomatic of a last breath, a last gasp of our inability to embrace change.

* * *

When James Traub met the same Yesenia I met much later, "a doll-like figure with a perfectly round face, perfectly wide eyes, and delicate, perfectly arched eyebrows," in the fall of 1992, she was attending a College Skills course in City College's Townsend Harris Hall (1994b, 84). Yesenia was a SEEK student who "had been speaking English for only five years" (76). At that time, she told Traub, "she was doing fine in class," but he "knew she was failing" (84). "She was hoping to get a degree as a physician's assistant, but she hadn't yet asked anyone how she could get into City's special program in the field . . . I could see that she was getting fidgety . . . In her mind, Yesenia was already with Taisha," her daughter (84), meaning that Yesenia was already giving up on her education.

Eventually, the fidgeting, the nervousness, *did* turn into what we consider *failure*. "Yesenia stopped coming to class. One day, she dropped by [Professor] Rudi's office with her baby, Taisha, but she refused to be drawn into conversation. Rudi never saw her again" (88). Maybe it was Professor Rudi's, and Traub's, manner that spoke foreboding to Yesenia: a very young mother only knows to protect her child, or was it that she was retreating to familiar things, things Yesenia knew.

The description of Yesenia suggests fear and trepidation, the acting out of her methods of protecting Taisha and herself. Why was Yesenia reluctant to be drawn into conversation? Was she indeed protecting something? What frightened her off? Yesenia was hiding. Something was obviously wrong in her life; the signs said this, though Rudi and Traub preferred not to ask questions to solicit what she knew. They closed her off. They did not *expose* themselves to her, making the atmosphere safe and conducive to an exchange. Intimacy was not invited. She was shown no method by which to express what becomes in speech the *impossible*. Nowhere in Yesenia's world is there a model for sharing, only for taking and for aggression. Traub and Rudi, who represent the institution of higher learning and the culture at large, successfully supported our society's propensity to close off and shut down, so she "refused to be drawn into conversation," as they refused her.

Rudi and Traub didn't know what to do with themselves in front of Yesenia's apparent confusion and despair; rather than admitting that the system is not tolerant of *difference*—of challenge—which would require astute reflection on the part of the participants who dominate and evoke change, they reacted with a punitive, unforgiving demeanor. A different, more creative approach would have changed the stringent roles Rudi and Traub blindly chose for themselves like soldiers following orders from a high command.

So, then, is Traub actually drawing a picture of *his* fears, as well as Rudi's? Is he acting in a way that supports the ideals of the institutions he represents, and that are represented in him? Isn't this what we have all been taught to do when faced with the unknown, with change? It's inculcated in our culture, as is blaming the victim.

> "If poor people behave rationally," says Lawrence Mead, a professor of political science at New York University, "they would seldom be poor for long in the first place." Many social scientists today appear to hold this point of view and argue that the largest portion of the suffering poor people undergo has to be blamed upon their own "behaviors," a word they tend to pluralize. (Kozol 1995, 21)

Traub, Rudi, *and* Mead failed; the institutions failed; we've all failed. We have failed Yesenia—and many like her. Failure has become a model, a standard to achieve. And she's blamed for it, as we also blame everyone else who is Hispanic or black or anyone with the slightest problem with Standard American English, even though these problems are also profitable, as is evident in the marketing of *gangsta* culture in music, videos, and movies; evident in the welfare state, which is not cleaned up or fixed, but used as political fodder. There's a large industrial complex built around the glorification of this type of failure ready-made for Yesenia to feel that she is not alone, that it is a sanctified avenue to take.[2] It's Yesenia's "refusal," not ours. Yesenia therefore understands failure, defeat, and punishment as the modes of a disciplined citizen. It's a self-fulfilling prophecy grounded in few or no expectations of certain people in our culture. No wonder she wants to run!

Higher education provides the ready-made language to accuse the student; this is then culturally supported, as in Traub's (1994b) *New Yorker* article which stands firmly against City College's attempts to address these inadequacies. Nothing is done, though the phenomena can be studied from afar and glossed over with glib responses, like the painted facade of the abandoned buildings in the Bronx shown to Kozol:

> The great problem with this society is that we don't give a shit about our children. That's where the problem lies. And by the time they get up here [City College] it's too late. (Traub 1994b, 90)

So we are left to follow channels, become frustrated, and complain, like Traub in *City on a Hill*. In our dissatisfaction, we want to look to someone, a vent for our feelings, our inadequacies, our failures as a culture. But no one responds, or else they respond with manufactured slogans for answers: "Just do what you can"; "One person can't do anything"; "They're all like this"; "They can't be helped." It's no wonder we lash out in anger. Scream.

By the time I met Yesenia at Borough of Manhattan Community College, certainly a demotion from City College by any standard, and two years after Traub's investigation, her experiences, the culture's ideas of moral absolutes, and Traub and Rudi had done plenty of damage. Yesenia was not a SEEK student anymore; she was now in REACH, a program meant to move mothers off welfare and SSI and into Human Resources Management. Is there an irony here?

I found Yesenia deep in the torpor of malaise. She had landed in yet another basic skills course, her hefty L. L. Bean backpack and large, three-ringed binder in tow. She still fidgeted, turning away when my eyes met hers. Where Traub and Rudi may have seen these as signs of indifference and inevitable failure or an unwillingness to participate, (Kozol's "Professor Mead Syndrome"), I took these to be an invitation to dialogue and a cry for help—*notice me*. This was her creativity, her *style: her way*.

I wanted to express myself to her correctly and carefully because I knew that "language is always a matter of force, to speak is to exercise a will for power; in the realm of speech there is no innocence, no safety" (Barthes 1977, 192). Yesenia's will to power had been squelched. It was a whimper. She wasn't doing anything in class. She sat, occasionally writing a sentence or two, but without substance. I sensed that I had to level the playing field to draw her out; she and I had to be, in her eyes, equally vulnerable for her to speak and eventually write. Vulnerabilities spark truths, I was certain. For Yesenia, I was still too much like Traub and Rudi, so I had to change.

I asked her to come to my office on the seventh floor of Manhattan Community College's mammoth campus on Chambers Street, in Tribeca. It was early fall and the sun was shining brightly; scattered, bulbous clouds floated against a blue backdrop. A partially opened window let in the sounds of nursery school children playing, car horns, the bustle of Greenwich Street at midday. Someone calling out; echoes between the buildings. Wind. We were already three weeks into the semester. Time was short. I had to act.

Hesitantly and awkwardly, Yesenia knocked on my opened office door, then smiled. She was nervous. She had on a denim skirt and jacket, and Timberland boots; she wore a touch of makeup for the first time. She wanted to be noticed, to look different than she did in class. It was as if she was coming to see someone she thought required special attire. She had thought this meeting through. Class is altogether different, in her mind. She imagined that something else, something perhaps more significant goes on in the office of *él profesor*. Yesenia had a sense of honor about her, and a sense of fear.

"Pase. Pase," I said getting up and gesturing toward a chair next to my desk facing me. "Come in. I'm glad you came. Have a seat."

She sat and looked around the room. The bookshelves caught her attention.

"Ju read all dis?"

"No. Those aren't mine. These down here are mine. Those up there are books publishers push on us to use in classes. We sell them to people who are in the business of buying secondhand texts. They come by a few times during the semester. Train money; lunch money. It's a racket. Publishers hate professors who sell their free copies to textbook wholesalers. Maybe we're producing too many textbooks? But that's another story."

"Du we *h*have to get one for our class?"

"No . . . no . . . no, we won't need one. Any readings we do I'll give to you. You don't have to buy anything. Didn't I say that already?"

"Ah, maybe. Per*h*haps . . . Good anyway. I *h*have no money."

"Yesenia, I called you here because I'm worried. I'm worried that you're not getting anything out of what we're doing. The semester is over before it starts and you have to get through this class so that you can take the regular English courses you need to graduate . . ."

Looking away; looking down, "I know." Then nervously, as if confessing a dark secret, she whispers, "I can't write." She looks around to see if anyone heard.

"What do you mean, you can't write? You've written."

"Not like da oders . . ."

"Everyone writes differently, Yesenia. This isn't a factory. I want you to write about what's important to you. What you know . . ."

"I *h*have noding to say."

"I don't buy it. Why did you come up here? I think you have plenty to say, but you don't know how to go about it. This is why you're here, right now. You want to know. I can see it! All we're doing in class is talking and writing about our experiences. That's it."

"But dey'll laugh."

"Why? Why should anyone laugh? They're worried about themselves. They're not worried about you. They won't laugh. Everyone in the class, even me, we're all struggling; we're all trying to get through."

"Ju? Ju're da teacher . . ."

"Yeah, I know. It's hard for me too; every class is different. Every day is different. I don't know what will work, what won't. I don't know if I'm doing right by you. It's very frightening. It's even more frightening when you realize that people, students like you, are listening, depending on you. So we all struggle, Yesenia. It has to be a combined effort. We have to help each other."

"I don . . . I don know . . . I do dink about dings, but I don know . . . I couldn't write at City. I left. I failed da same course . . . Exact same . . . Remedial . . ."

"You're not going to fail this one."

"How du ju know?"

"Because *we're* going to make sure you don't."

How can I put my trust in you? Yesenia was really asking. *How can I trust you to be able to see in me something I cannot? Who are you, saying these things to me?* she was wondering. *Who are you, really?*

Looking at Yesenia sitting now more sedately before me, her round, delicate eyes pleading for answers, I wanted her to realize, as Allen Ginsberg sings in "Ode to Failure" (1985), that "many prophets have failed"; indeed, *failure*, viewed correctly, *naturally*, as Emerson's "tiles and copestones for the masonry of today" is a source for creation. Out of life, out of the past, comes the new, artfully constructed. This is what teachers of writing can do: we can create an atmosphere whereby students can re-create themselves artfully.

I had to prove to Yesenia that this was possible; I had to give her an example. I found that if I could reconstruct myself for Yesenia, she might begin to understand how our past, our failures, our misconceptions can lead to aesthetic refabrications of our desire for an identity—to a poignant reconstruction of an individual's will to power.

I began to look at how I had gotten here, to this point, to BMCC, Yesenia, and the others. "Thinking through the ways in which past and present experiences inform the other," says Ruth Vinz (1996), "no teacher is free of history and context. From this, I assume all teachers are constrained and emancipated by their places of experiences as well as the challenge of possibility" (87). I would add: not just teachers, *all of us* are "constrained and emancipated," so it is ludicrous not to use *our* "places of experiences . . . as the challenge of possibility." I wanted to "enable" and "facilitate" her "readings" of herself—herself as text (97).

"Reflection upon situationality is reflection about the very condition of existence, critical thinking by means of which men discover each other to be 'in a situation,'" Freire reminds us (1972, 100). Tragically, we have come to see this notion as some sort of misguided liberal agenda that is destroying the very fabric of our culture; however, we fail to realize that Freire's idea is at the core of Western civilization and can be found in Socrates and Aristotle, in Marcus Aurelius and Quintillion. It is quite conservative thinking. In fact, it's global thinking, found in the Tao and the Hindu, the Islam as well as our Judeo-Christian tradition. Freire's neoclassical argument is unifying, embracing!

So why are we so eager to deceive ourselves—and our students? Why are we so eager to work with subterfuge when history tells us otherwise? Why are we working against Nature?

I was seeking to make Yesenia active in her own learning experience, active with herself. I, too, wanted to have Yesenia create her own personal or subjective meanings from her experiences and from the texts she read (McCormick 1994, 30). In essence, Yesenia had to find her voice, then use it. I was subscribing to Frank Smith and Kenneth Goodman; to David Bleich, Norman Holland, Louise Rosenblatt, and Stanley Fish; and to James Britton.

To open her up, to let her *see* herself, I was certain she had to *see* me; she had to *see* how I learned, how I had come to be in front of her: where my voice comes from. There was a circle around Yesenia and me now; it was apparent and waiting to be filled:

> Our life is an apprenticeship to the truth that around every circle another can be drawn; that there is no end in nature, but every end is a beginning; that there is always another dawn risen on mid-noon, and under every deep a lower deep opens . . . There are no fixtures in nature. The universe is fluid and volatile. Permanence is but a word of degrees. (Emerson 1960, 168)

Learning is like the universe, fluid and volatile, *and* frightening then. It was evident in Yesenia's expectant gaze—and my hesitation. We could both feel a certain pull, a visible deepness suggesting that even though there are "no fixtures in nature," we were experiencing something new, different. We were attentive to our misgivings. It was indeed a beginning, so I started with a story about a little boy, a grammar school age boy, from another place and during a vulnerable time, before he became a teacher.

* * *

Marcelo stood out in grammar school. He wore a black leather skullcap tightly strapped to his chin to protect him in case of a fall. From his knees to his feet he was encased in steel braces fastened to cumbersome black leather ankle-high boots. He dragged himself across the school yard by pulling on steel crutches. He had a grueling rhythm: pull, drag, hold; pull, drag, hold. When he pulled, his legs followed and his feet dragged slowly behind as if they weighed tremendously. Momentarily upright, Marcelo held his balance and inhaled deeply before beginning the process again. Two long lines in the dirt traced where he had been. The kids in the school always ran past him on their way to *futbol* (soccer) games and marble games. Marcelo arrived much later, after everything was well underway. Occasionally, a teacher walked with him.

Marcelo's physical weakness was matched by his vehemence, his tenacity: a willingness to be confrontational knowing he was protected by the kids' awareness of their physical prowess, his physical weakness. Marcelo rendered all kids helpless, like himself, making them self-conscious about their maneuverability. He did this by challenging everything that was said; every utterance became a point of contention the kids had to consider, but not react to physically. He removed the physical comfort little boys enjoy. He acted as self-appointed referee of *futbol* matches and judge at marbles, indifferent to loud displeasure when calls were questionable.

"No, that's no foul," he'd yell from the sidelines, waving one of his crutches. "Stupid, how could that be a foul?" he'd threaten; then pull, drag, hold all the way to the infraction. The kids waited, wondering how much time they had to the end of recess and the bell, thinking, *hurry up*, but gathered around Marcelo anyway. "You're so stupid. How can that be a foul?" Marcelo would say, then meticulously recount the incident. "It's a drop ball. I'll do it." Leaning on his crutches and holding the ball with two hands—"Ready?"—he'd quickly let it go between two players. The game carried on, moving away from Marcelo; he would pull, drag, hold back to the sidelines, glancing over his shoulder after every hold.

Marcelo had no problem voicing what he saw. In a heated dispute as to which marble was closest, everyone deferred judgment to Marcelo's crippled torso barely able to bend over the tight circle of intense marble hurlers. It was as if everyone believed that Marcelo's disability gave him insights other kids didn't have. They believed that he could see what they could not because of his paralysis.

There was another boy in this grammar school, though, one who played *futbol*, tossed marbles, and watched Marcelo with a kind of resignation, a fear-at-a-distance kind of interest that was personally confusing: he didn't know what to make of Marcelo; he didn't know what role *a Marcelo* played. So this little boy simply ran past Marcelo, as did everyone else; it was best, he thought, to go with the crowd. There is comfort in the crowd when fear of the unknown precipitates.

But on one particular day, when this boy was doubled over, intensely engaged in a close game of marbles in the school yard, he noticed the rhythmic pull, drag, hold of Marcelo, the cloud of dirt behind him, inching toward the game. On this day, Marcelo looked larger than usual, more ominous, his rhythm more purposeful. He even thought he noticed a smirk on Marcelo's face, a smile. The boy quickly looked away, trying to lose himself in the marbles before him that he couldn't see anymore.

Marcelo was coming for him—coming to expose him, he thought with certainty.

"Hóla."

Everyone kept playing, accustomed to Marcelo's late arrival. But this other boy, the one who looked at the cripple with resignation, felt Marcelo's eyes on him. He glanced back and nodded.

"Héctor, hóla," said Marcelo with a smile.

The boy knew what was coming.

"Hóla," he said. "Is your father okay? Is he alright?"

The game stopped. The players looked dumbfounded at their friend. "Your father? What's wrong with your father? What happened?" Héctor's friends asked.

"Ah . . . ah . . . nada. No pasa nada. Está bien." Nothing, said the boy; nothing had happened.

"No?" wondered Marcelo. "Isn't your father sick? Didn't he have to go to the hospital? Paralyzed, right? It *must* be your father. My therapist, Marta, she told me specifically, *Héctor's father, one of your classmates.* I think we'll have the same therapist."

"No . . . no . . . no . . . My father's fine. It's someone else," small Héctor said immediately.

"How could she be mistaken? How could she have made such a mistake? If you say so, then. You know . . ."

Marta wasn't mistaken; neither was Marcelo. Héctor didn't know where to hide from Marcelo, from the image of his father with black leather skullcap, braces, and crutches. . . .

Poliomyelitis—polio—is an acute viral disease, most common in infants, which had been Marcelo's problem, characterized by inflammation of the brain and spinal cord, resulting in paralysis. Héctor's father was similarly paralyzed. He spent several days fighting for his life in an iron lung; from there, lying prostrate, he planned the rest of his life. He would never be able to drag himself across the ground as Marcelo did; the polio had been much worse. Héctor's father never walked again and would witness life from a wheelchair.

Héctor couldn't let anyone know. He stopped having friends over and only went out if he was going to someone else's house. He lived a secret life, as if his father's wheelchair was a confinement for him, too. He wanted to shut the doors to his father's paralysis, believing it would be construed as his own—a weakness. The private had to be kept from the public, Héctor decided. How frightened he was! This fear would last a long, long time—into adulthood.

*   *   *

"Wow . . . dats ju. Da small boy, Héctor," said Yesenia with aston-ishment. "What *h*happen then?"

"My father was in the military, the Argentine Air Force. He's an en-gineer. So they gave him—us—the option of going either to London or to the United States—here in New York, for rehabilitation because in those days—we're going back some thirty-five years now—Argentina didn't have the means to rehabilitate him. Then there was hope for my father. But I think he knew all along he'd never walk again."

"*H*he estill doesn't walk?"

"No. It's been years. I don't think my younger brother even re-members our father ever walking, that's how long it's been. My brother's a grown man with a family now. The Rusk Institute, it's now the Tisch Medical Center at NYU—you know where it is, right?—they got him so that he could do everything for himself, and occasionally stand with crutches and leg braces. Sometimes he'd drag himself about the house. But he's given that up now for some time."

I sat back and watched Yesenia relax. She giggled nervously, nodding.

"The public, being out in public display—it's so scary, Yesenia."

"Jes."

"But we all have our fears; we all have those very dramatic in-stances that make us who we are, that make us unique. These give us character. This is what binds humanity. Everything else is nonsense; it's neon."

An ease passed over Yesenia. What I could see in myself, and what I immediately sensed in Yesenia was a release from the fear created by the encroaching public scrutiny that tries to bind us into some collec-tive idea of wholeness, of morality, of normalcy.

I now have come to realize that the small boy confronted by Marcelo had learned to use his fear of the public, brought on by his fa-ther's illness, to redefine himself as the teacher that sat before Yesenia's

darkness: the teacher's history and Yesenia's history were interconnected at that precise moment.

Emerson's lessons were here, too, but framed in a new way. This
was improvisational, meaning that I relied on intuition—the *art* of
teaching—and this, more than anything else perhaps, opened up the
atmosphere, changed the climate and made the inner, private self more
hospitable, more capable of transacting and negotiating the powerful
outer, public world.

The most difficult part of the art of teaching is developing the confidence to act intuitively; sometimes, though, as in Yesenia's case, the
situation demands it. I felt the urgency, the need to begin to open *new*
avenues for Yesenia's expression. What was discovery for me, could be
a text for Yesenia: she could read me to read herself, thus re-creating
herself in new and different ways.

It's as Umberto Eco tells us in *The Role of the Reader*:

> The addressee is bound to enter into an interplay of stimulus and
> response which depends on his unique capacity for sensitive recep-
> tion of the piece . . . As he reacts to the play of stimuli and his own re-
> sponse to their patterning, the individual addressee is bound to sup-
> ply his own existential credentials, the sense conditioning which is
> peculiarly his own, a defined culture, a set of tastes, personal incli-
> nations, and prejudices. Thus his comprehension of the original arti-
> fact is always modified by his particular and individual perspective.
> (1984, 49)

Yesenia had been in confinement too long. She stopped fidgeting.
Her dark eyes didn't waver; they looked right at me, sparkling. Forgotten were Traub and Rudi; she had proven Professor Mead wrong as
well. Yesenia's force gave that sense of power and mystery one feels at
the edge of a massive ocean: the onlooker is transfixed with mixed feelings of seduction and foreboding as the waves lap the soft sand. Her
force came in waves of exhilaration, despair, and need. She had ideas,
I could sense it; she was drawing parallels, defining her culture.

The circle we made was begging to be filled; it was beckoning.
"Writing will take you the rest of the way, Yesenia," I said to her. "Our
relationship is now different."

"Whata ju mean?"

Just as a classroom comprised of welfare mothers looking for better
lots in life requires special, and perhaps bold, untried methods, within
this circle "a Yesenia" always emerges, requiring yet further plunges
into the teacher's sense of self within the context of the teaching art.

The classroom is therefore the only *free* space our culture has for
opening up these raw lines for teaching, learning, and experimentation; the classroom is the only space where we can respond to these
kinds of needs.

I was hoping that Yesenia would recall our meeting once back in the classroom; she had time to think about it. Writing, good, solid reflective writing, would help her see the circle within her; it would help her close the circle, unite the missing links. My responsibility was to provide the proper prompts: "Fold new, clean sheets of paper in half, please. This is the start of an assignment. On the left side, above everything, print 'Inner.' On the other side, print 'Outer.'

"I'm going to give you approximately twenty-five minutes for each section. Let's begin with the Inner. Listen carefully and begin writing when ideas start to filter in. I'm going to give you a series of prompts, or suggestions—motivations. Ideas to help you get started. I will keep repeating these and when you feel comfortable, when something sparks, start writing and don't stop until I say 'Stop.' Don't even look up. Write and write and write . . .

"Ready? Think back. Close your eyes if it makes it easier. Think back to your lives and recall an incident that you sense really changed your life. What event do you think changed the way you look at the world; the way you understand the world? What event sticks out in your mind as the single most important event of your life to date?"

By the time I ask this last question, and repeat the others all over again, sometimes in different, softer ways, even Yesenia is writing. I move slowly, for a few minutes, around the circle, repeating, ever so softly, the prompts, then quietly sit at a desk within the circle and begin writing myself. It's good work to write together:

> *The class is engaged. There isn't a sound. Only breathing. Much has happened to this class so far. I feel as if they're loose. I think they are somewhat comfortable. They look forward to these assignments. They responded quickly to the* Inner *prompt. Do they have a lot to say? Was it easy for them to grab something that altered their perspective on life? Will everything they write be tragic?*
>
> *I worry about Yesenia. I wonder how she will feel after taking this chance. She's been beaten down so . . . They all have . . . Speaking to her, though, seems to have brought her out a bit. At least she's writing—and without hesitation.*
>
> *I was certain of my shortcomings in trying to fully realize what it is to be a young, single mother of color, like Yesenia, in an inhospitable climate. This was beyond my grasp. Besides, I'm a man. I am Spanish, but white, often mistaken for an Italian, a Greek, or anything. (Is this a sign of how collective racism is? Why are we so adamant about quickly placing individuals into categories, classifications and the like?) I'm hardly ever regarded as Hispanic, which today is synonymous with dark or black, of a low socioeconomic class, and exploitable.*
>
> *I had to cross this bridge with the class: an apparent misnomer, a white, educated, middle-class Spaniard had to meet twenty-two welfare mothers, ages twenty-one to thirty-seven, with a cynical view of any institution, halfway to trust. How much work our culture costs the teacher!*

A teacher has to use everything he/she has to bring out the student. It's exhausting. It's like laying brick. In Bootstraps, *Villanueva [1993] says that the teacher is the new blue collar worker: overworked and underpaid. I'd add: under-respected! What will happen to a society that does not value teachers, that does not value learning, real learning and not just "for a job"?*

"Stop!"
Yesenia's private, *Inner* world:

I cant speak about one thing. There many. No two. My mother was my best friend. When I came from Puerto Rico I lived with my mother in an apartment. It's on 3rd Avenue and 101 St. The area is not good but I like living with my mother. We stay inside alot and we talk. She watches my daughter and help me raise her. We like to watch TV programs. Like the stories in the spanish station.

When my mother died I feel all alone. I don't know what to do. I have no one. I'm scared to speak to anyone in the apartment. They want to get in your business. I hate that, I'm private. So I stay with my daughter inside all the time. We play and watch TV. Its so hard to get her to sleep. She stays up sometimes and we watch Letterman.

Yesenia's *Outer* world, the description of things outside the hearth, hints of which appear in her *Inner* and thus demonstrating an overwhelming power, is colored by the urban blight of crack dealers, petty thieves, and violence. Interestingly, too, Yesenia equates her *daughter's father*, her phrasing, his comings and goings, to her *Outer* world. Her *daughter's father*, one of New York's finest, a New York City Police Officer, and *a Jew*, she says with pride, as if this demonstrates she has somehow conquered her *nuevayork*, arrives unannounced and takes Taisha on some weekends. If he so desires, Yesenia tells us, he also stays in her apartment for as long as he wants, sleeping with her, then leaves for undetermined periods. He gives her money erratically, but only for Taisha, an instruction, Yesenia says, he constantly repeats. And he hits her.

Yesenia is on *welfare*, receiving money to attend my class; she is bound for a government job in human resources, though we are experiencing massive budget cuts in this area—in all areas. She feels the irony of this: "The government dat wans me off welfare is cutting back so I won *h*have a job. I may not even graduate because there's no money. Whattam I goin to do?" This is an abuse of trust given to people in moments of despair; it is the disciplining of citizens that can't battle the state: Yesenia only has "exchange value"; she is merely a transaction in a city that routinely adjusts to the ebb and flow of power. She "re-presents" the means of power production: she is there to be observed, but not to be granted certain freedoms. Yesenia is incarcerated.

After condensing and synthesizing the *Inner* and the *Outer*, and after scrupulous editing, whereby Yesenia concentrated on the simple verbs in her sentences to achieve significance and labored with a dictionary, this is what she wrote:

> We all must face death. Death is part of life. But we all don't know exactly how to live with it. Death is natural. It's like birth. Birth and death are the most important parts of a person's life. We all must face death, but we don't know how to deal with it. This means we have to learn about death to be able to understand what happens to us after a loved one passes away.

At the end of the assignment, just before handing in their packets of drafts, I asked the class to write a reflection about their writing. I asked only one question: how do you see yourselves as writers now? Yesenia responded:

> I thought I had nothing to say. If I'm pushed I write. I think I can write but I have to get better at it. I don't know if I like this yet. It's hard, but it's good for me.

Yesenia passed the dreaded and paralyzing CUNY Writing Assessment Test—the WAT—and moved to College Writing 101. She came to see me several times during the following semester, but not to show me any of her writing. "I'm doin good," she'd say. "I can do this by myself." I would confirm this, from time to time, with her teacher: "She's okay. Not the best, but she should be fine." Yesenia was blending; she was a student. She passed 101 too, with a C.

The next time I saw Yesenia was at BMCC's graduation. In blue cap and gown, she came running up to me, Taisha in tow with flowers in her hair. "Thanks," she said. "See, I did it. I'm graduatin. I'm goin to get a job, then go back to City. I wanna finish. Didn ju say it was very important to finish?"

Notes

1. The Generation X label is instructive here. X, as in "X marks the spot," Queequeg's signature in Melville's *Moby-Dick*, or as in Malcolm X, suggests loss, the unknown, and the desire for identity. Interestingly, Generation X has been so labeled by the dominant class, suggesting an industrialized—and banal—creation of a category associated with decadence, revolution, and disgruntlement; this is the aesthetics of revolt commodified so as to pacify. The dominant class has not forgotten the '50s generation that became the revolutionaries of the '60s. Too much turbulence, they say. The dominant class has figured out that by creating a category—Generation X—it can pacify through the marketplace: you can look like a Generation Xer, so you don't have to act on it; buying is the acting. This then translates into passive, nonquestioning students in the classroom; however, all these students want, as is evident in their earrings, their baggy pants, their colorful T-shirts and caps worn backwards—are ways

to channel a sense of loss and fear, a sense of wanting to belong, of wanting to be thought of as unique. They have something to say, but find no avenues for self-expression in the institutions that inhabit them—and that they must inhabit. Generation X is silence and sameness brought to an aesthetic level—and sold. It is profitable. This then doubles as insecurity; they've been brought to their knees before learning to stand. In many ways, Generation X is in deeper trouble than those students who come to higher education from adverse and foreign backgrounds that include not only cultural deficits or misunderstandings, but socioeconomic ones as well. These particular students are struggling to survive and have learned to challenge authority by questioning its efficacy. Generation Xers think they have won, but they have lost. Generation Xers are blinded by the glitz and glitter of the marketplace; however, students from the underclass understand that there is a strict class structure myred in an old world hierarchy—and it's this hierarchy that defines access to wealth and power. Underclass students therefore struggle to redefine themselves.

2. On March 9, 1998, in the *New York Post*, Bob McManus reports that the New York City Board of Education has lost track of 56,000 students. Payments to the board are based on "complicated, attendance-driven formulas that boil down to this: Every time a pupil misses a day of classes, the Board of Education is docked one pupil-day's worth of state aid." Thus the motivation is to count as many students as possible—or tolerable—present. "Hundreds of millions of dollars in state education aid hangs in the balance . . ." This is the anatomy of corruption extending from the State all the way down to New York City's Board of Education. Fraud, of all varieties and types, is rewarded. But we never stop to *reflect* on how this translates to the students, especially the 56,000 missing. McManus's own perspective, for instance, is not even remotely concerned with the students, but rather, with how this action will "feed into the profound suspicions of the city harbored by increasingly powerful elected leaders from upstate. How credible now are city pleas for fiscal 'fairness' as the current budget debate proceeds in Albany?"

Chapter Three

Out of Life, Out of the Past

The wide-eyed little boy Héctor, *me*, presses his nose against the airplane's lozenge-shaped window. He is trying to feel the cold. Far behind is the torpor of Buenos Aires in January, and now, sitting next to his father, the ice on the window speaks of a frightening unknown that lay ahead. He wants to run from it, yet he also wants to "hurry up and get there." He is caught in an unmitigating web.

He hears his grandfather's anxious voice: "*Americanos*! Van a volver cómo *americanos*!" The grandfather was afraid of Americanization—assimilation meant ruination. He was afraid the family would abandon him, be lost and different. In many ways, the grandfather was right; he was abandoned and, at least for Héctor, there is loss and confusion.

What is grandfather afraid of? What is America? Are we so different?

In Argentina the little boy and his younger sister played games, trying to imagine the sounds of English. Gibberish, guttural sounds is all they spoke. They looped together squiggly lines on a page and labeled it "*inglés*"; they listened to their father, the only one in the family who spoke English, and imitated the strong nasal sounds so foreign to their romantic language. They would laugh, tensely and fearfully; they couldn't get the *inglés*. Spanish is melodious, a song, and English is preciseness, piercing: this is how the languages sounded to the little boy.

A few nights before their departure from Buenos Aires to New York, the entire family—grandparents, aunts, uncles, cousins—sat beneath a starlit night and attempted to give texture to the unknown. The maternal grandparents' home in Rosario had a large courtyard in its center that etched a bright, velvet sky. Beneath, the family sat at a long and noble table: the cooked chickens' roasted skins glistened; candles lit the linen tablecloth and gave it a soft, inviting quality, a warmth;

dark bottles of wine were lined in a neat row across the length of the table; *Cinzano and soda in siphons.*

Noise and laughter.

The grandmother described how funny it was to watch the little boy round up the chickens in her backyard earlier that day: he chased them to her, and in the tumult, clouds of dirt whirling about their feet, she grabbed an unfortunate one that wandered close to her ankles, quickly twisting its neck in a fluid, circling motion, and dropped it into a steel vat filled with scalding water. She showed the boy how to pluck the chickens' feathers; they pulled out their innards, then stuffed them.

They reminisced; laughed nervously; imagined. They tried to push away the encroaching inevitability, though it persisted, coming closer and closer, until nothing else was visible.

Looking out the airplane's window at New York's Idlewilde (Kennedy) Airport, life in Argentina is but a blur, unreal, someone else's. The little boy is mesmerized: concrete and snow and gray; red trucks, yellow trucks, blue and white trucks—all sizes and shapes—race about; planes and more planes. *Do not get up from your seats until the captain turns off the light,* is the first English sentence he hears, and he doesn't understand; his father pats his thigh, *Todo va ir bien. It will be okay. It will be fine, you'll see.*

It truly is another place, another land, forebidding and alluring, like the ocean, large and plentiful.

His heart races.

The airport: noise, crowds, people pointing: *this way, here;* Exit; No Exit; no Spanish; English only; bustling; huge carts like small cars to the little boy moving luggage about quickly; men in uniforms opening suitcases and running grubby hands through everything: *my underwear, mamá;* shops and more shops and more shops: everything's for sale; flags; reds, whites, and blues; *no espeak* English. *Aerolineas Argentinas.*

The cab: monstrous cars with chrome and lights and wings; speed and fury; the tick-tock, tick-tock of turn signals; lanes and white lines on the road; tall, ominous buildings; gray, and more gray; dirty snow high on the sides of roads; cars stuck in snowdrifts; cold, freezing, penetrating cold; plow trucks; a tunnel under the water? *what if it floods?* tolls?

Then, Manhattan: alien; noisy, and indifferent; traffic stopped, jammed; no sky, bits of sky; no sky again; pigeons; white smoke from the ground? people bustling and rushing and holding hands over mouths and newspapers around necks; ear muffs; wind in icy, stinging gusts; black snow; more cold; more people, crowds of people; more pigeons; the Empire State Building, Times Square and Broadway; Macy's and escalators; *wow!* sirens and air raid shelters; *the Russians are coming!*

Motion. Speed. Plenitude.

From the window of the Martinique Hotel, the little boy watches people in dark coats rush about in the snow and gray-black slush, crossing Greeley Square, scattering pigeons. So many pigeons in the square, perched on Horace Greeley and on the ledges of buildings, in the air. Throngs of people force their way into the abundance of Macy's; others come out with large bags filled to the top.

But something more powerful then the motion and speed outside the Martinique Hotel compels the wide-eyed boy inside: Television — where abundance is aestheticized, made into art and morality.

In Argentina, there were hardly any televisions in 1960, so the immigrant family didn't own one, having only heard of their mystique. They didn't even have a phone, though they were middle-class and lived in pristine Cofico, *un barrio* — a suburb — of Córdoba. Only a single family in their neighborhood, the Rectors, had one. Consequently, Matilde Rector knew everyone's business because everyone used her phone; she would run down the tree-lined Segunda Lavalleja, delivering messages to different neighbors. *Teléfono, teléfono,* she'd shout. *Mensaje.* Matilde was communication central. Matilde and electricity were the extent of the technology.

The family is split once more, the father admitted into Rusk Institute and the rest moving into an eighth-floor apartment in middle-class Riverdale (the Bronx), the Palisades visible at a distance. The black-and-white Zenith television distracts them from the difficulties of their sojourn in America. Solemnly, elegantly, it sits on a chrome stand in the living room. It is their most vital object, a valuable eye into this foreign land — and they honor it by bringing the family together to watch *Popeye* and the *Mickey Mouse Club*, the *Ed Sullivan Show* and *American Bandstand*, and the little boy's favorites, *The Flintstones* and *Bonanza*.

Before bilingual education appeared, television taught the immigrants English. The entire culture paraded before them: salesmen and appliances; Westinghouse, *you can be sure*, GE and Texaco; *American Playhouse*; cigarettes — *have a Lark, have Lark* — and TV dinners; violence and civil rights and war. John F. Kennedy.

"This is the new President of the United States," said the father. "Kennedy. John F. Kennedy, the first Irish Catholic President. He has asked Americans to help their country, rather than taking from it. He said, 'ask not what your country can do for you — ask what you can do for your country . . .'"

"I love that," said the mother immediately captivated by the romantic allure of Camelot. "Argentina needs someone like Kennedy. What wonderful words."

"It's a very important time for Americans," said the father. "A new age. He's looking to transform everything. Kennedy is creating a *new society*, a *new*, more vital culture. It's an exciting time to be here."

The little boy hears, but doesn't understand his father. He doesn't know about America and *los americanos*. Everything *is new* to the little boy. The city, its speed and aggression, subways, above and below ground, the people, supermarkets, all America speaks a loud and powerful language that is decentering. The signs are illegible, literally: he is an outsider, yet there is no escape; he *has to be*—in America.

A nightmare: the little boy feels paralyzed, not knowing what is being said, not knowing how to act, how to be, what to do when people speak to him, so he stares back—silent. He can only smile and shake his head, *no*. They laugh, look the boy over, up and down, then shrug their shoulders saying things in unpleasant tones.

I felt it. I felt it within my silence. Silence became my companion; in it, I observed, listened, repeated. The aloneness became overwhelming at times. I learned to be with silence and aloneness—the outsider, always, to this day, the outsider.

I was learning to write, though I didn't know it yet. I was learning to see.

Thirty-five years later, he can still feel the kids' eyes focused on him back then, feel their power on the first day he entered St. Gabrielle's, in 1961, in Riverdale, a Catholic school just a couple of blocks off the Henry Hudson Parkway.

Crew cuts and Brillcream, *a little dab will do you.*

Brown uniforms and penny loafers.

He doesn't have a uniform, or loafers, and wears a funny-looking wool sweater knitted by his mother. No one has sweaters knitted by their mothers, only bought ones, from Macy's probably, he thinks.

Stares. Smirks. The power of the group!

He wants to be his little brother, who is too young for school and stays home with his father's aunt, Nené.

Introductions into public American life.

"This is Hector Vila, our new student from Argentina," says the nun.

He hadn't experienced the Americanized Hector, the strong H sound overwhelming the more sensuous, fluid Spanish, *éctor*, accent on the *é*; the *i* instead of the appropriate double *e* sound in Vila (Veela: *see*); the *g* of *g*entle, Argentina, instead of the Spanish *j* sound we hear in *h*eavy and *h*eight. Everything bastardized, changed, more pragmatic—the American way.

"Welcome, Hector," the class joins in.

He hears his name in whispers and murmurs repeated as he walks up the isle to his seat near the back of the class: *Hector? Hector! Hector Heathcoat . . . haha . . . Hector Lopez . . . Pancho . . .*

"Where's Argentina, anyway? Is it in Africa?"

The public can overwhelm the individual, driving him into silences. Retreat.

On the first day of his new experience, the nun signals for him to come to the board with other students. Waving, gesturing, like a cop directing traffic in a busy intersection, she repeats, "Come up, *Hector*. Come on up. Come."

Slowly, hesitatingly, he eases out of his private desk and walks to the public board; he senses the student's eyes, their grins: the foreign kid on display.

He stands facing the board, unlike the other five students poised with chalks in their hands, and tries to lose himself in its blackness, tries to enter it and pass through it. He witnesses the students' confidence, his fears, and stares into the blackness of the board. He feels different.

Dios.

"Spell, *cat*," says the nun.

A flurry of activity: everyone writes. He presses the chalk to the board, trying to will something, to understand, but nothing comes out. He looks at the other students, again. He can't decipher anything. He makes like he knows but can't recall. The nun turns his head and, with her index finger and a smile, taps the board before his eyes. Immediately, he hates her.

"*Dog*," she then says.

More activity, more writing. He can see that the others have two words, one beneath the other. In front of him are merely a few dots reminiscent of the games he played with his sister, nothing more. Squiggly lines. He draws from what he knows, thinking that *something*, anything might spring forth and satisfy the nun's scrutiny.

Sweat.

They are watching.

Murmurs.

"Quiet, please. Quiet. You should all be writing in your books. I'll be checking. Now, *Bee*. Spell, *Bee*."

He is lost, totally. He has an overwhelming feeling of aloneness. Tears well in his eyes: he clenches his fist and bites his tongue.

He thinks of home, of Cofico and friends left behind who he understands; his grandfather and *las Pampas*; *Spanish*. Television.

He damns his father.

He wants to go back. Run.

But *Hector* can't.

Where would *Hector* run?

Hector has to be here. There are no choices, except surviving this. No exit from performance!

"All right, everyone sit."

He tries a half smile when he faces the class and shrugs his shoulders as if saying, *I know I don't know. What do you want me to do?* They are humored by his oddity, the foreigner.

Harlequin.

During recess, in the school yard, like his sister, he wanders. Kids circle around, speak and gesture. *Yes, Yes,* he says, grinning. *No entiendo.* And nods pathetically. He stands against the fence, watching kids jump rope and play hopscotch and stick ball. Occasionally, a brash boy comes over.

Taunts.

He can tell by the laughter and the stares.

They think his silence a weakness. But his silence is a form of study. He listens intently, watching curiously, every gesture, and in overwhelming aloneness repeats words, phrases, eventually dialogues. He tries these out on his sister; compares them with what he hears on television; struggles with billboards; studies cereal boxes: the lexicon.

I started to feel less alone. I was not only learning a new language, I, too, was learning how to write. And I was learning how to learn.

But first *H*ector has to exist as if he lives in a cell, as if he's been jailed, incarcerated by everyone's marginalization of him—because he is different, a foreigner; he exists in solitary confinement and within his own imagination laboring to understand the signs being presented to him.

It is claustrophobic. It is hard to breath.

Days last an eternity, and recesses even longer. He hates recess. He is vulnerable there: alone, in the privacy of internal dialogues, yet totally in the public. He is negotiating, learning that the public and the private, as Cornel West says, are intertwined, perhaps one and the same. He is reluctant to give up his sense of the private, inner self for the public's demands. Hector wantes to impose himself, (h)*éctor*, create himself, not be created.

*   *   *

One day, a boy that was always taunting him came over. By now, some things he understood: *Hey . . . Wait . . . Come over here . . . Wanna play? . . . Shit . . .*

"Hey, SPIC," the boy said menacingly. "You're a SPIC, right?" he repeated, smirking.

*H*ector wasn't ready. He became flushed. Surprised. Threatened.

He didn't know if it was the tone, the word or both. Spic. He knew it was directed at him, he was certain, feeling deep down inside that it wasn't good. Evil. The taunt was defining him in a public way—and violating him: a public violation.

Humiliation based on fear of the unknown: "He's a Spic everybody."

He lunged at the boy and hit him and hit him and kept on hitting him until a monitor separated them.

They were taken to Mother Superior. The menacing boy spoke and Héctor couldn't. So for two weeks, the boy went to recess and Héctor spent time in Mother Superior's office sitting, silent and alone, doing penance. He knew it was punishment, but found it to be a sanctuary from the tension of the school yard. It was another type of solitary confinement; it was a physical confinement that accented his psychological one. But he welcomed this time to ponder, decipher words on book jackets, listen and repeat dialogues in his imagination. He grew fond of the respite found in his forced solitude, his aloneness.

Tragically, the little boy was left back. He repeated first grade because he didn't speak English, hadn't made substantial progress. Like Richard Rodriguez in *Hunger of Memory* (1982), the little boy felt "extreme public alienation" (3), a "victim of two cultures" (5): in the intimacy of the home, everyone spoke Spanish, *español, castellaño*, forbidden to speak English, fearing the children would lose their *natural* language; everywhere else, it was English, *inglés*.

But the Spanish world grew increasingly smaller; English came in through the front door, television, books, and school—American noises. English overwhelmed; it dominated. The children began speaking Spanish to their parents, English to each other. Now as adults, when they speak on the phone, or at family gatherings, the children speak English to each other and Spanish to their parents, when spouses are not around. Spanish has been successfully driven to the margins, though it is still at the core of their being.

So it went, for nearly five years, one side of the little boy's education: taunts; aggression; fear and embarrassment; Mother Superior's office; penmanship; spelling bees; diagramming sentences; straight lines to the bathroom, to the lunch room, to confession, and to church; communion; the clicker: genuflection—in unison. The rhythms of order.

And always silent, the outsider, defining within himself a world he could live in.

This is how writing began: noticing that he was always the outsider, he needed to re-create himself.

*   *   *

The other sides of the little boy's education were the Metropolitan Museum of Art and the Rusk Institute.

"This is a portrait of Sesostris III," instructed his mother. "It's from about 1850 B.C. Try to imagine that. A long, long time ago, way before Christ was born. Look at how real it is. It's from what's called the Middle Kingdom, a time of great change. Look at it."

"From Egypt we get writing and arithmetic," his father also instructed. "That's when history began, with the invention of writing five thousand years ago."

A cultured family, a privileged immigrant family: the mother was a teacher and the father an aeronautical engineer who graduated with honors from Argentina's Air Force Academy. He was a propulsions expert, commanding knowledge of weapons systems and thermodynamics; a film addict and a colorful, funny storyteller—a critic—who brought his son along to the cinema, sometimes to two a day, out of one and into the other: *Tarzan, Laurel and Hardy, El Cid; The Longest Day; The Train*, with Burt Lancaster. The boy's mother, whose parents were reluctant to send her to college, hitched rides with girlfriends into the Rosario countryside to instruct illiterate peasant children in a hut erected out of wooden posts and pampas grass. An occasional cow would wander in and disrupt their work, done on small, portable chalkboards; no texts: the teachers taught from the heart and listened, without pay. But in the city, Rosario, she tutored students to pay her tuition. She was *called* to be a teacher, which means that she was dedicated to bringing out the best in students, what they knew. There was never any question: she was doing Freire before Freire knew what he was doing. *Conscientização*.

In the Metropolitan Museum of Art, a public place, the mother, and the father in a wheelchair, gathered their children in a tight, intimate circle before history's artifacts and exposed them to the chronicles of cultures, from the dawn of civilization to the modern, and speculated about the future: the Ancient World—prehistoric man, the Egyptian, the ancient Near East, the Aegean and the Greek; the Christian and the Byzantine; the Middle Ages; the Renaissance; and the Modern World, the little boy's favorite and what he would study in graduate school: neoclassicism and romanticism; realism and impressionism; Postimpressionism.

Before *multiculturalism* came into vogue because America had become so internalized and indifferent, compartmentalized, narcissistic, and consumed with itself—*Amero-centered*, not Euro-centered—the little boy, the silent, observant outsider, was exposed to the interconnectedness of civilizations. He was being taught to be a citizen of the world, not of a place. Humanism. The father's polio forced this on them.

He was also being taught how to teach, how to integrate disparate elements for creative results.

"What do you see here? *Que ves?*"

"Ah . . . ah . . . When I get close, they're pieces of colors. Small dots. When I move back, slowly, the dots come into focus and there's a painting where there wasn't one before. It's a show. Yeah, *Side Show*."

"Here, what do you think?"

"It's . . . it's like a photograph. So real. That's a painting? I want to touch it."

"*Muy bien*. It's Caravaggio. He was different for a Renaissance painter. So realistic. It's a religious theme with very *real* characters: armed men, the Roman tavern, and poor people. Look at Matthew's gloomy face. Very *real*. It's the lighting that makes the painting appear so sacred. See, the light comes from heaven. Remember Michelangelo? There's an influence here. Painters borrow from other painters; one generation learns from a previous and the new generation tries to use what they learn from the past, but in new ways, ways that demonstrate how the new age has changed."

The little boy was learning to *read*, to *reflect*, and to *criticize*; in the meantime, both the mother and the father whispered history into his ear: *this was done between 1887–88; it was a time of transition and experimentation; Europe was the center of the world and the United States was growing, becoming the power it is today, after the First World War; people weren't comfortable with conventional ideas, they mistrusted and looked for changes.*

He was learning to negotiate history with image. He was learning languages, their uses and implications—their force. Aesthetics and phenomenology. He was learning the importance of metaphor; that life is represented aesthetically: the Body of Christ; God the Father, the Son and the Holy Spirit; original sin and venial sin; Edouard Manet, Monet, and Degas; Rodin's *The Thinker*; Van Gogh, all of him; and yes, Pablo Picasso, a Spaniard.

Everything could be used aesthetically to make a statement, metaphorically; objects are subject to interpretation, layered in meanings, he was certain, and this was fortified by supplemental interpretations: the Guggenheim, the Museum of Natural History and the Museum of Modern Art; music on the Fisher stereo, complete with radio: Caruso and Frank Sinatra, Harry Bellafonte and Chubby Checker; Handel, Mozart, and Haydn; Beethoven; the Supremes and Motown; the Beatles.

The little boy's original sense of America's cacophony was slowly levigated by art. His parents prodded him to see, to reflect, and then to speak, to explain what he saw and why.

Interpretations.

He relished the subjectivity of it all; it gave him significance. They let him come to culture and history—to civilization; in it, he could place himself. He was attracted to his parents' teaching methods. It was inculcated in him, and natural. He learned that sculptures, paintings, and music are windows onto the world, which the outsider needs to rearticulate himself. It was—and is—an organic process.

He was less alone in his imagined partnerships with art; however, these relationships also punctuated his problematic existence, framed by different realms which pushed him further to the margins: old, European-like Argentina and new, aggressive America; the inner sanctum of home and the public demands of school; natural Spanish and forced English rules; art and history; mobility and paralysis—dichotomies and ironies.

In each of these places, he began to feel somewhat at home, but also a foreigner, like an intruder or a tourist—passing through. Belonging and not belonging. Fractured. He was neither *in* nor *out*, but somewhere in between. This made him unsure; he became angered by his vulnerability—always angry. Confused.

The weekly subway trips into New York City to see his father at the Rusk Institute further confused his identity—and fueled his anger.

The Rusk Institute, a surreal place. In the lobby, off to one side, was a greenhouse. He would sometimes wander into the lush, humid room that housed a fountain and a parrot, and imagine himself in distant, exotic lands. (The little boy was also learning how to run, how to find places for escape from himself, from the confusion he felt.) It was a way for him to leave the Institute while he waited for his father to wheel down from the fourth floor on the way to the dreaded cafeteria: the Saturday family outing.

He hated the cafeteria. It was a haunted house of quadriplegics, paraplegics, amputees; nature's accidents and deformations; hydrocephalics: monsters and misfits in bibs, food and saliva running out of their gaping mouths and down their chins. All around, the sounds of choking, the sounds of misconnections struggling for logic—the sounds of despair for normalcy denied.

The boy couldn't eat, pushing the food down, gagging, teary-eyed. He would try to smile at his father, who demanded his son respect and accept the deformed—and look beyond. But his stomach hardened.

He had nightmares, tossing and turning and covering his head with his sheets, trying to dislodge the disfigured, who encroached on his mind.

His father's fourth-floor room was the Latin quarter: a Colombian who suffered a gun-shot wound to the spine (paraplegic); a Venezuelan, paralyzed from head to toes because of an automobile accident (quadriplegic); a Puerto Rican with a broken neck (quadriplegic); a Guatemalan electrician whose one arm and two legs had been fried by hot wires (amputee). They were all here, looking out over the East River, to learn how to live with their *handicaps* in a world inhospitable to the nonwalking, the non-whole and incomplete.

On the second and third floors of the Rusk Institute, the boy sometimes accompanied his father to watch him lift hand weights, stretch himself on pulleys, and drag himself with steel braces across parallel bars. In the swimming pool, his father was lowered by a sling and a lift into the water that replaced the steel braces and the crutches and, finding partial liberation from paralysis, was able to slowly float about as if in suspended animation.

The Rusk Institute taught the *handicapped* how to put on clothes by themselves; how to go to the bathroom (by themselves); how to lift and pull their wheelchairs—those that could use their arms—over hostile curbs; how to drive a car with hand controls; how to cook; how to be independent, yet live with unfathomable physical dependencies in an indifferent world: how to become *un*-handicapped and approximate normalcy.

It was at the Rusk Institute—another marginalizing place, another place that drove the boy further into his imaginings, his aloneness—where the boy was again redefined.

"Thank God your father has a son with wide shoulders," the mother would always say.

He learned how to live behind his father's chair, pushing it first within the Institute, then eventually throughout New York City. *Watch out for people's legs.* The boy became a wheelchair aficionado: he pushed his father over New York City streets, in department stores, in museums. First, he stretched his neck and head to peer over his father's shoulders, then over his head, and eventually he towered over him. He saw the world of the disabled; he learned how his father thought, staring into the back of his head, listening and observing the logic of it all. An education.

When the father began driving, it was the boy who put the foot rests, the left-hand arm rest, seat cushion, and entire wheelchair into the trunk of the car, a Mercury Comet—their first American automobile. Then he sat next to his father. The Comet opened their horizons; it became new legs for the father, and the rest of the family. They went upstate, hugging the Hudson River, to Hyde Park to visit F.D.R.'s home, a family hero, not because he had been President, but because he too had achieved in spite of his polio; to Connecticut and Candlewood Lake; all the way to Florida, Miami, and Palm Beach—twice; to Canada; to Washington, D.C. (to the Smithsonian, of course).

All the time, it was the boy who pushed his father and received a bird's-eye view of a world of boundaries—and the tremendous struggle to overcome them. He, too, realized that the physical boundaries designed by *the normal* were, in fact, metaphors for greater and more subtle intellectual and spiritual boundaries.

"Everything would be so much more comfortable, even easier, if architects and builders would build things for the handicapped," his father said. "The non-handicapped would find things much easier for them too. The trouble is they don't know *how* to think like someone who is handicapped."

The boy learned. There was a logic to what his father said: the New York City streets and sidewalks, always obstructed by water or snow and ice or garbage, the entrance to buildings, the awkward public bathrooms, and the always-too-narrow doorways required forethought before every action—seemingly for everyone. People acted sometimes in unconsciously cruel ways. The boy noticed how the indifferent, physically mobile ran into each other at street corners, and pushed or shoved or tripped over his father, then looked down at him as if it were his fault, as if he shouldn't be down there.

From behind the wheelchair, the little boy learned how disabled *the normal* are, how indifferent and callous, and how *un-disabled*, how really *normal* was his father with his lifeless legs. Handicapped Only: the boy hated these signs, this inaccurate designation. It was a lie.

His father's polio opened his eyes and changed his vision of the world.

Years later, after a family luncheon at the Plaza Hotel, now a man with wife and children, *I* was very conscious of how easy and automatic it was for me to go to my father when it was time to leave. My father seemed to expect it, though he didn't say a word. He was very much at ease with me behind him. *I* was easy with it. This familiar discourse was comfortable for both of us.

We went out the side door of the Plaza, its gilded front entrance too inhospitable for wheelchairs, and crossed the street to Central Park, where the rest of the family waited amongst the phaetons. It was a bright fall day. The air was crisp and the sun warm on our faces. Leaves were on the sidewalks; the smell of dung and horses and sweet sycamores hung in the air. It was romantic, genteel. It was the grandchildren's turn to be introduced to the Met: Caravaggio was there.

Strolling easily up Fifth Avenue, I suddenly became very self-aware; my entire life, like a movie, passed before me in a flash, a single image. There I was, a *big* man, as people like to say, slightly bent at the waist, leaning over my father's gray-haired and balding head, pushing his wheelchair up Fifth Avenue. All around us, the kids, my brother and sister, spouses—everyone—was involved in their own conversations, or chasing after the young ones. And I was behind my father, with my mother to my left, on the side closest to Central Park, walking beside me, her right arm linked through my left.

It felt bizarre, surreal—not because this was new to me, it was not—but because I had never realized the significance of it before: mother was strolling, as she had done so many times in her life before polio struck, down a boulevard in Rosario or Buenos Aires with my father, her husband; however, now, and many other times like this one, my father and my mother were carrying on silent rituals from their past through me. Old anger began to rumble.

I was involved in their intimacy. This had been my life, this had made all the difference in my world: the father, the mother, and the son in the middle; not quite inside, not quite outside, always in the margins. It's inhospitable in the margins.

The marginal existence is an accurate description for my life. I feel *almost* at home everywhere—but not quite. It's a life of incessant searching for a secret, lost other, out of the past. It's *a life* that has been lost because it was replaced by another, the one behind the chair in America.

I remember hearing Yves Montand and Maurice Chevalier on the Fisher stereo and my mother taking me in her arms and showing me how to dance. *Lead*, she'd say. *You determine where to go. Listen to the music.* Even then I realized that I was a surrogate for my father. *El hombre de la casa*, my grandfather labeled me when my father became ill. But those were hard shoes to fill, my father's, for this naive *man of the house*, the little boy. I was only six then. I've never come close. Still haven't. He set a high standard, a difficult standard—a common dilemma experienced by the first-born male in a Spanish household.

Or perhaps I have achieved different things, in different ways? Perhaps what I have achieved has been to learn to break away from the triangle.

I lived in the seams of everything. Upon reflection, however, these aspects of my life—the harrowing early years of *non*bilingual education at the hands of unforgiving nuns (so much Catholicism, so little Christianity); the intimacy of the public Met; the Rusk Institute—these vastly different cultures nourished in me the sensitivity and insight to notice and appreciate students who themselves were marginalized, lost, meandering. I can sense where they have been fractured and disenfranchised. I am also certain of their limitless potential. I'm open to it, or better said, I've been opened to it.

We can all find this within ourselves.

I feel comfortable and at ease with the black, the Hispanic, and the white middle-class student who lives in what I identify as a *middle-class coma*: a lulling to sleep by complacency with lower standards and consumerism. These students, in turn, identify with me, though we have enormously different backgrounds: theirs limited, and mine arguably privileged. How is this possible? By means of mutual respect in an open classroom that they must dominate, define, and inhabit. I don't lie to them about their limitations; instead, I demand standards and realistic expectations. No kid gloves here, just honesty and good listening. Work.

Looking back through my history, all seems so simple and innocent now: tragedy was what brought my family together, and me to teaching; tragedy changed my family and opened up my vistas. Ironic. Of course, I wasn't aware then that I was actually witnessing how tragedy creates; how it nurtures the imagination of those willing to openly accept drastic change and new impressions; how self-sacrifice—the *opening* of one's self *to* another—actually brings out the best in both, which is what Freire argues, as has Gramsci before. And Plato before that. But it's a sloppy process.

I now realize I was being formed to be a teacher on the day my father took ill. Circumstances formed me, and brought me here, to teaching. I'm convinced I can't do anything else. My family is an animated one: storytelling, impassioned political discussions, humor, and intense listening are always vital to our tight circle; we draw each other out. But the tragedy of my father's polio broke this circle; to regain it and to understand it, to live in its nurturing safety again thousands of miles away, without an extended family and in a foreign culture demanding assimilation for survival, required a troublesome journey, characterized by alienation, loss, and confusion. Disenfranchisement. Every member of my family here in America has had to remake himself and herself.

Self-empowerment, learning to create, I now know, requires the momentary loss of self—a letting go, a free fall—and then an arduous yet rewarding journey to redefine what was lost—the self—in imaginative ways. Something new is created. It's an endless cycle repeated throughout one's life. It's a cycle that must be re-created in the classroom so that both students and teachers can examine it and determine where exactly they exist in it. This is how we learn, and how we then revise ourselves. It's never easy, often painful—it's always a process.

Chapter Four

"What You Know, I Also Know . . ."

Am I the sea, or a sea monster,
that thou settest a guard over me?
When I say, "My bed will comfort me
my couch will ease my complaint,"
then thou dost scare me with dreams
and terrify me with visions,
so that I would choose strangling
and death rather than my bones.

Job, 6:12

Excess of loquacity can be a sin, and so can excess of reticence. I didn't mean that it is necessary to conceal the sources of knowledge. On the contrary, this seems to me a great evil. I meant that, since these are arcana from which both good and evil can derive, the learned man has the right and the duty to use an obscure language, comprehensible only to his fellows. The life of learning is difficult, and it is difficult to distinguish good from evil. And often the learned men of our time are only dwarfs on the shoulders of dwarfs.

Umberto Eco, *The Name of the Rose*

New Yorkers often flee the city in August. The heat and humidity are suffocating; every gesture, every move is arduous and heavy. The atmosphere is inhospitable. People tend to stay within themselves and dart their eyes away if they momentarily meet another's. Some individuals, preferring to stand alone, make their way to the edge of a subway platform, impatiently lean over the tracks, and look down into the black hole, trying to conjure up a train with their anticipation. They're anxious.

Anxiety breeds in the city: there is no escape from anxiety—or from environment.

In Washington Heights, or anywhere in the Bronx or Brooklyn, people lean out of windows like birds waiting for a breeze. The heat forces people out, and they must face each other: some sit in lawn chairs in their buildings' alcoves or beneath the brief shade of a singular tree across from their front doors because some of the parks in these areas have been colonized by drug dealers and their clients. Nobody needs hassles, especially in the unforgiving weather of New York City's late August.

Emerging from the dark and dank subway station at Broadway and Chambers Streets, sweat on my brow and shirt stuck to my body, I faced a Hudson River I couldn't see but knew was there, somewhere behind the impregnable, gray curtain of haze and smog—and gasped for just a hint of fresh air.

Nothing.

Moving closer to the river, still no air.

I sauntered, composed, visualizing my life-yet-to-be at Borough of Manhattan Community College (BMCC) rising slowly out of the dampness: a challenging unforgiving, even alienating and menacing presence daring to be conquered.

It could swallow a person live, I sensed. Yet I felt strangely at ease, as if I belonged here now.

Across the street, on West Side Drive, Stuyvesant High School stands, open and inviting. New. A postmodern icon. In contrast, the presence of Manhattan Community College looms ominously, as if required to warn the fortunate attending Stuyvesant: if you don't do well, you could end up here. Thus, in this last corner of Tribeca exists a microcosm of New York City: *the haves* and *the have nots,* grazing shoulders on their way to school or home, living separate lives side by side. Thus, callous indifference greases the rusty gears that keep New York City running.

At BMCC's entrance I stood before Icarus, an imposing, gold statue that was cast at the Vila foundry in Spain. Irony, omen, or both, I thought: this is where I must be now; all signs point to this. Icarus stands stalwartly at the college's doors to warn us of our tendency to abuse knowledge for self-gain.

Inside, I was startled by the rush of stale, cool air, the recycled climate of the college's inner core that sustains life throughout the year—or that hinders it by rechanneling, and making worse colds, flues, and various respiratory ailments. There's no escape; most windows are sealed. The recycled air carries the residue of its past and it can hurt you. It's always a problem at BMCC: there's either too much air or not enough—and it always contains some contaminants.

In our postmodern zeal to live in a sterile environment, the reverse is true and we have become more vulnerable to the tyranny of infection and disease in what we ironically assume are sterile environments.

"You have an ID?"

I explained to the security officer that I was here to get photographed for an identification card and to pick up a schedule of my fall classes—just a few days before they were actually to start because I was a last-minute hire, brought aboard near the beginning of the term. With no time for preparation, I wondered if it was all going to be improvisation. More than likely. I was just going to try to survive.

"Sign in. There. Good luck getting through."

Registration

Closed Courses

Cancelled Courses

Problems

Bursar

Beneath signs leading to more signs, thousands of students lined the halls, the stairs, and the theater, on the last day of registration, to get into *any* class, handle problems, get signatures—to understand *the system*. Get through. From the looks on their faces, some seemed to have been standing on line for hours, perhaps days; they had the look of resigned frustration, of going from line to line, only to be told that they needed prerequisites, they didn't have the right *paperwork*, they needed yet more signatures.

You'll have to go back, then stand in line again because you missed a step.

No, no. You can't take this course. You need that one first, then you can take the one you want. Besides, it's closed. You'll have to choose something else.

Lines, lines, and more lines; more paperwork; more signatures; more conditions.

I made my way through the sea of dazed students to the escalators and the seventh floor. English Department. Another line to see the department chair.

I needs to see the chair. Are yous the chair?

The system is a monster grasping loose prey in bureaucratic tentacles, and if you're caught, then you're lost, devoured—dead.

"Oh, hi. You made it," said the English Department Chair with a smile and a chuckle. "Welcome. It's usually crazy around here this time of year. They want to get into classes that are closed, so you keep telling them 'no,' and they keep insisting. What are you going to do?"

he continued, waving his eyes over the expanse of students lined up to seduce his approval.

He handed back a piece of paper to a young student. "There's nothing I can do," he said to her and walked away, towards me.

Dumbfounded at his sudden disregard, she stared at his back and gasped, "But . . . but . . . I . . ." Stunned.

"Let me take you downstairs and get you through this mess or you'll be here forever," he said to me, leaving the dejected student standing paralyzed. Other students were lined up behind her. They all looked at us walking away. Hope was leaving. Things were looking bleak, said their faces. Chaos would ensue, surely.

I watched the young student look at us and couldn't help feeling that she blamed my sudden presence for her depressed condition. Somehow, I was certain, she saw me as part of the problem that was preventing her from getting what she needed. It was the way she frowned at us—at me. *Were we involved in a conspiracy?* she must have thought. *Were we involved in some sort of private language that excluded others—her?*

I was now one of *them*: I created hurdles and conspired to raise them higher.

I realized that if this student, left gazing blankly, was to end up in one of my classes, we were already off to a bad start. She didn't trust me; from a different world, she supposed I was accustomed to a language different from hers. She would think I was closed off to her.

Barriers created by the system, give each and every one of us, students and teachers alike, particular identities as we respond to demanding conditions and prerequisites. They make learning tense and difficult, the classroom foreboding and alienating. The system establishes hierarchies meant for discipline and indoctrination, not for learning: and we go along. Through not-so-subtle lessons, we learn how to behave; how we must think; what language we are to use in any given situation. I immediately became a problem added to the many problems this student already had and was trying to solve without much success.

Alongside poverty and despair, I learned, sickness is pervasive among the students at BMCC. A host of debilitating physical ailments— chronic depression, asthma, HIV, AIDS, chronic flus, anemia, intestinal ailments, and viruses of all types—intrude on their learning too. (Never sick, I was seriously ill, needing bed rest, three times in two years while at BMCC.) It's in the air, the contaminated atmosphere.

"Excuse me," said the chair. "Excuse me. This is a professor. We have to get him photographed right away. Sorry." My escort took me to the front of the Identification line. All eyes were on us.

How come they get to go up there so fast?

At the front of the line, a young student was about to sit and be photographed: another dejected student; another obstacle in her long day; another hassle. And outside there was still that heat.

Perhaps Umberto Eco is right. How do we determine good from evil among the educated? How do we define "good" and "evil" in the postmodern experience of callous indifference? Some of us do indeed find comfort in "an obscure language" that is comprehensible "only to [his] fellows." But this marginalizes other learned people, namely students, who come to education having been realized through their own languages, their own means. This is threatening to us, so, we insecurely jeer at them, mock them, and blame them for their ignorance of our ways. We become "only dwarfs on the shoulders of dwarfs," and education ceases.

How much of what we do, as teachers, is teaching through negation? How much of what we do, then, is discipline—and not learning?

My ID card photograph shows a dazed and confused individual, a foreigner overwhelmed by a foreboding environment. But I learned something that day: every student would have this experience in common: they've been pushed around, manhandled, and made to feel dejected; they've been overwhelmed by *the system*; they know the system, and others like this one.

Systems need to *use*, and even devour, great masses of people; it's what keeps them going, it's their food. By design, a system requires components to sustain it so it can continue negotiating. The components in a system are expendable, replaceable; systems operate within a devour and purge mentality: the legal system needs the criminal; the economic system needs unemployment and poverty; the medical system needs the pharmaceuticals, the pesticides, the multinational agribusiness corporations, the infirmed. We've created a culture for these transactions to occur.

Borough of Manhattan Community College needs the poorly educated, dysfunctional student who comes out of an ancillary system: the depressed, economically challenged neighborhood, riddled with crime and disease—prerequisites of the legal system and the economic system. It's a vicious, brutal cycle of despair and deprivation.[1]

The teacher, unknowingly, or perhaps even willfully in many cases, becomes the person in the middle or, more accurately, the first line of defense, the frontlines: s/he seeks to reverse the cycle; enlighten and appease; comfort, but not commiserate, and find the mean. Equanimity. The teacher is involved in spiritual healing because her students are the tragic victims of our culture's misprisions.

"The teacher of the coming age," says Emerson, "must occupy himself in the study and explanation of the moral constitution of man more than in the elucidation of difficult texts" (1960, 93–94). In no other profession is this possible; the teacher is most capable of carrying this mission forth.

I wondered how I could use this philosophy as a basis for creativity; the students' experiences and my own had to blend, synthesize, come together in an effort to define ourselves within this monstrous structure. We had to *transcend* it. This would then be the creation of something new, something quite different: the articulation of ourselves within a system that is vehement about defining us; we could *read* and *reflect* on our roles within systems, any number of them.

Everything at BMCC, I sensed, is about the survival of the system, and the students are merely tools for that survival. Nothing else, or very little else, matters, except, perhaps, for one's personal aggrandizement. Are all systems and the institutions that house them the same? How, then, could these hidden voices of the students, and my own voice, be heard from the bowels of a monstrous institution like BMCC?

The students at BMCC have been properly institutionalized; they are *institution people*: recipients of welfare, inner-city public education, public hospitals, and the legal system—*the law*, or more precisely, *jail*. These students, who live within one monolithic institution or another, move from one to another, or exist within several simultaneously— welfare check, guaranteed student loan, parole officer, are indeed the products of a tremendous bureaucracy that feeds off their needs and de- sires. These students have been branded: requirements, rules and reg- ulations, and plenty of paperwork have placed a mark—a blemish, per- haps—on their existence, as have poverty, violence, and hopelessness.

Institutions are objects that negotiate perceptions—*all* percep- tions. They have become a pestilence afflicting intellectual and spiritual growth. These students, these citizens, are fully governed. They are la- beled, watched, stamped; they are quantified; they are incarcerated and tested; and they are segregated. This must produce a particular per- spective; if these perspectives are used, then *institution people,* people who are living from institution-to-institution, must contain a particu- lar understanding, knowledge, that speaks about harrowing conditions in our culture. These students must know everything about the world we live in; they see it all. They see truths; they see hopes; they see faith. They see justice and injustice; "good" and "evil," I was sure, they knew quite well. In essence, students were saying to me what Job said, "What you know, I also know . . ."

If institutions are defining them, I believed, students from the "underclass" must also be defining and characterizing the world we live in; in turn, society uses what they articulate as weapons against them, failing to see their goodness, open hearts, and longings. The doors to education and hope are now really closed—firmly sealed and air tight. This is the *under*side of a vertical civilization.

These students become the "sea monsters" Job speaks about; they are the ones who wonder why we "settest a guard" over them. We do not trust, so we guard and incarcerate. Who don't we trust, though? Them? Ourselves? Job said something else, too: "What is man, that thou dost make so much of him, and that thou dost set thy mind upon him, dost visit him every morning, and test him every moment?" (7:17) Are we not actually the ones incarcerated?

I wondered, what would happen if those who have always been guarded were liberated and made free to speak and create and visualize themselves independent of their surroundings? I was certain that the curriculum I and my students needed—that we yearned for—was motivated and defined by our mutual experience *in* institutions—*the system*. I sensed that such a curriculum would open vistas and provide opportunities for all of us to *re*articulate ourselves along lines analytical and critical, not only of the institutions that house us, but of our responsibilities within them as well.

In *The Culture of Reading & the Teaching of English* (1994), McCormick suggests that there is a "need for students to analyze the sites in which their values are formed to recognize that their readings of texts . . . have larger social consequences" (63); that it is "possible for students to develop the capacity to learn about and interrogate the historical conditions in which texts were written and have been interpreted" (59); that their readings have been socially and culturally manufactured, as have their texts; and that students can take up active roles in *re*-creating themselves, and therefore culture.

In a different way, though emphasizing the same notions, Sven Birkerts tells us

> In the humanities, knowledge is a means, yes, but it is a means less to instrumental application than to something more nebulous: understanding. We study history or literature or classics in order to compose and refine a narrative, or a set of narratives about what the human world used to be like, about how the world came to be as it is, and about what we have been—and are—like as psychological or spiritual creatures. The data—the facts, connections, the texts themselves— matter insofar as they help us to deepen and extend that narrative. In these disciplines the *process* of study may be as vital to the understanding as are the materials studied. (1994, 136)

I became certain that deep within these students lay hidden voices that bespeak truths concerning our culture's pursuits, our civilization's march toward humanism.

*   *   *

Remedial writing is an indoctrination. They're unruly and improper. They don't know how to be students yet. I was told that *this* was my job: to make students out of nonstudents; to soften their harsh edges for other teachers up the ladder. To make them *proper* students. *You'll see how it is. Wait.*

Just do what you want, some make it, others don't. There's really no one way. It doesn't make a difference what you do.

Bleak.

Was I hired because I'm big and strong and could probably *police*? Was that my job, to *hold* students in place for a while so that they weren't in other places where they could get into trouble and cause different kinds of strains on the system? Was BMCC a holding tank, English a kind of supervised midday stroll in *the yard* circumscribed by a tall barbed wire fence?

I looked around for help, a way out of the role of guard in a panopticon. And I found four types of remedial writing instructors: (1) the intimidated and, therefore, totally noneffective and harmful teacher, who allows students to overwhelm the classroom through aggression and disruption, thus convincing them that education is bogus and empty of promise; (2) the intimidating teacher, also noneffective, harmful, and dangerous because there is so much hatred in this classroom, so much resentment, that students learn to reject and mistrust any representation of knowledge and experience a violent *mis*representation; (3) the "white liberal" Cornel West speaks about in *Race Matters* (1994): a dangerously subtle racist who thinks only in salvation terms and believes himself/herself to be essential in raising the "underclasses," which s/he does by patting students on the back, letting problems go, and telling them "just express yourself." S/he does irreparable damage by (re)presenting deceitful images that reenforce dysfunctional and costly dependencies; and (4) the overwhelmed, dedicated, and well-meaning teacher still trying, after many years, to negotiate between sensitive, insightful, teaching and a ravenous bureaucracy, but experiencing a type of burnout or tunnel vision, and looking for a way out— retirement, intellectual sleepwalking—in between bouts of depression that are accompanied by deep philosophical and spiritual introspection: "Where did I go wrong? This is not what I had in mind when I got into this."

Remediation is confusing. No one is really certain what to do, not the administrators, not the teachers, certainly not the students. We have Shakespeare scholars, Milton scholars, microbiologists, Java programmers, systems analysts—but we have no remediation scholars.

What is the role and function of remediation? How is it that we've reached a point where remediation is believed to be essential? Are schools failing, particularly public schools, to educate our students for college? What role do economics play in creating, aiding, and abetting the remediation underworld?

In the purgatory of remediation everything is visible, exposed: the ugliness; the beauty and magnificence; the doom, gloom, hope, and aspirations all pass through the remedial class. It's emotionally draining.

There's a lot of suffering and anguish, some joy and astonishment, frequent surprises, and a good deal of talent, too.

These students' personalities are being depleted; they all wanting life but different lives. They want to embrace change, or at least find a way to become accepting of drastic change. They need change and they can sense their need.

They haven't realized that the acts that have comprised their lives and that they perform daily for survival, their efforts to "get ahead," are affirming, are the foundations for change. They have been instructed through negation and rejection that they aren't worth much, that their acts are meaningless and they don't know much about the world they live in. That they need us. The decrepit state of their schools, their overcrowded and stifling learning environments, and the despair in their neighborhoods are signs of slavery—of lives of servitude and incarceration and of a system dedicated to disciplining.

We conceal from these students, the people of the "underclass"— and from ourselves—how much we need *them*. We deny that these students are forming us as well, reformulating our entire culture, in fact. Instead, like an assembly line, we churn out a compressed world characterized by intense anxiety and the pressure of failure. Failure dominates, and is a way to slow the wave of inevitable change. Nature is running its course; the *under*class will eventually become the *over*class. What have we shared with them? What have we created as governance and education?

"You *need me* to pass the WAT. If you don't pass the WAT, out you go, back to the streets. What will it be?" Choice and democracy in education, there it is. Then, we punitively pack remedial classes with twenty-seven to thirty students when there should be no more than fourteen or fifteen. Nevertheless, all the students in the class try and work on themselves, *tryin to bettah ouselfs,* they say. Energy and persistence are required of everyone, so each student devising his or her own method of getting attention in the overcrowded remedial underworld where survival—and it's all about survival—in this context extends our Darwinian sense of it.

Some students call out for attention by being chronically absent. Do we fail them? How are we to respond to their cries for approbation? How do we learn to hear their unique, sweet voices overwhelmed by cacophonous despair?

The unexpected—chaos—is the most dominant characteristic of a remedial writing class. Energies are disparate, flying in all directions; students speak to each other at any time; they get up, leave, or walk across the room, speak to someone else, and return. *What he say? Whatta we doin?* They call out, eat, drink, go to the *bafroom.* In, out; up, down. Noise. Chaos.

It is an exhilarating experience—refreshing and stimulating—if a teacher is open to it, feels her way around, and allows herself to be within this confluence, allows these energies to govern directions for intellectual and spiritual inquiry through writing.

Nothing is to be feared here: this is a teaching and learning environment, a healthy terrain, though we've been lead to believe otherwise.

The "wise man," says Emerson, "must feel and teach that the best of wisdom cannot be communicated; must be acquired by every soul for itself" (1960, 279). "Trust thyself," he says in "Self-Reliance" (1960, 247).

Confusing and chaotic energies are actually voices asking to be heard, channeled, and *re*directed. It's a wonderful place for a teacher to be: the students at BMCC taught me about teaching, about myself. They have affirmed my own personal acts. Their sounds became my sounds; they spoke to me about how they wanted to be taught. This happened through writing and dialogue. They lead and wrote; I followed and recorded what I experienced, what I heard.

For instance. Tamika, who on the first day said she was "a model" and "I has a chile," would coyly bat her eyes, tilt her head, and smile sheepishly. "Mistah," she'd call me, "I don unnerstan wha you wan. Is this it?" Tamika would then show me a beginning of something written in gigantic, infantile lettering but in complete sentences and logically thought through, though it was not very analytical or critical. Tamika always understood, but was reluctant to trust herself, a sign of having been abused somewhere in the education system.

"What else can you say, Tamika? Can you describe this condition, this tension? Where do you think it comes from?"

Tamika did pass the WAT and went on to Freshman Composition. Throughout, she never stopped calling me "mistah," or "hey," and even went on to ask me, at the end of the term, "wha was yo name again, mistah hectah, victa, something like dat?"

Glenda perpetually pouted, like a disconsolate child. "No. I can't," she'd say. "No. I don't want to. No."

"Glenda, please, I'm asking that you revisit a situation that you find significant in your life. Something that changed the way you think about something."

"No." More pouting.

"Glenda, Glenda, Glenda," I would repeat softly, like a father to a child, then I would slide into Spanish (bilingual education?), her language of intimacy, smile, and say, "Glenda, *I'm* only going to read it. No one else. I'm doing this so I can see where *we* can work to improve. If you go to a doctor and there's something physically wrong, you're not going to tell her to guess, are you? You're going to let her know, to the best of your ability, what you think ails you, right?"

Glenda had no father and was the youngest in a very large Dominican household. I became her father figure: I scolded her, pushed her, frightened her with her own reluctance. Threats, teaching, cajoling, and, finally, work, in Spanish and English, all functioned together to produce and develop clear Standard American prose. She needed someone to help her transcend her cultures and pass the dreaded WAT, which she did.

Oscar was a scrappy, good-looking, sensitive young man who blew out his knee playing baseball in the Dominican Republic, where dreams of American baseball and Nike contracts border on the religious. He was a pitcher.

"I coulda played. Cincinnati was lookin at me. I threw har, man, har. Yeah. They said I had good speed."

Now he was working his way through the "remedial underworld" with another dream in mind: "I'm gonna get married to my girlfriend, open a business and have a family. I'm gonna make sure my kid study first, then play ball. I shoulda done that. Now look at me." We talked sports, family, and what it takes to "make it." Oscar liked to see the obstacles, the things "a man gots to do," so I would describe for him the harsh realities and violent demarcations that exist in our culture. "It don matter what *blanquito* does cause I'll be ready. I can do anythin, man. Go ahead, tell me what to do, no matter. I'm gonna make it."

Marcia had a daughter attending an affluent, suburban, private college in Westchester County—thanks to New York State's Higher Education Opportunity Program. Mother and daughter were both freshmen, though the mother was mired in the oblique "remedial underworld." My suspicion was that Marcia was "learning disabled," though no one had seen it appropriate to approach her. She couldn't write a word; everything was misspelled; she couldn't take direction; she never completed a single sentence, though she firmly believed she had said a lot; she never completed more than four or five lines of symbols, not words.

In the middle of class, during a discussion or when students were working on the board, or with me individually, Marcia would simply get up, walk to the front of the classroom where I was standing and speaking, whether to the class or with an individual, and interrupt.

"You needs to sign this for me," she demanded as if no one else existed.

"Marcia, we're in the middle of a class. Can you see I'm explaining something to everyone?"

"Ah-ha."

"Marcia, is this appropriate?"

"What that mean?"

"Look at the way the class is flowing, what we're doing, what everyone is involved with. Can you see the energy? Is this the time to walk up here and ask questions about an unrelated matter? These are your classmates, and you're interrupting them. Besides, don't you need to know what I'm saying, too?"

"Yeah, but I needs this signed. They axed me."

"Can't it wait?"

"No. I haves to take it down now."

"Why not after class?"

"No. Now."

I would sign and she would leave.

And at the end of the term, she couldn't understand why she didn't pass the WAT. "I been to every class, why can't you pass me? Is not fair. I worked hard," she said, tears welling in her eyes. Marcia would take Remedial Writing, English 090, two more times, never pass it, and leave the college. I tried to get her tested for learning disabilities, and she did speak to someone, but the means were not available for her. She was lost, never to know how she could, indeed, learn. But she had dreams.

What are *my* responsibilities to Marcia? To this day, I am unsure. I don't know what else I could have done; nevertheless, I feel that somehow I failed. But at what?

If any of these students were to have a chance beyond the CUNY Writing Assessment Test and the dreaded English 090, then I had to do something other than "teach to the test"—or police the classroom. If, indeed, my responsibility was to get these students ready for "other" courses, "other" teachers further up the education ladder, I was certain that I needed to create a learning atmosphere that was active; that would allow each of these personalities to flourish; that would channel these vibrant energies into an inquiry concerning the ideological apparatuses in our culture that coerce us into roles; and that would provide opportunities for the students and myself, to assert our identities onto the production of history and culture. Otherwise this task is left to the James Traubs of this world.

I needed an atmosphere that would facilitate transcendence and that each and every one of us could enter to gain an understanding of our culture. I wanted an atmosphere that would move all of us toward intellectual autonomy so that we wouldn't have to delegate our decision making to "career intellectuals."

If the institution promoted *indoctrination*, then we were all going to discover, define, and criticize our own positions with regard to these governing ideologies. We were going to teach ourselves how to see ourselves and encounter real, historically situated cultural differences and linkages.

Says Antonio Gramsci in *Selections from Political Writings (1910–1920)*:

We need to free ourselves from the habit of seeing culture as encyclopedic knowledge, and men as receptacles to be stuffed full of empirical data and a mass of unconnected raw facts, which have to be filed in the brain as in the columns of a dictionary, enabling their owner to respond to the various stimuli from the outside world. This form of culture really is harmful . . . It serves only to create a maladjusted people, people who believe they are superior to the rest of humanity because they have memorized a certain number of facts and dates and who rattle them off at every opportunity, so turning them almost into a barrier between themselves and others. (1988, 57)

In 1916, was Gramsci already forecasting America and its system of education? Have we Americans become lazy and lackadaisical because we have grown comfortable with(in) our reliance on a self-made image of superiority that is founded on "weak and colourless intellectualism"? (57).

I knew that I had to try to turn this around; I knew that my students had things to say; and I knew that if I were to prompt them to reflect and to recollect, then what they knew could be a bridge into literature, or at least into the canon, a bridge that could begin to contextualize their lives.

What I wasn't expecting was how much their work, their struggles, would affect my own insights into teaching and learning and writing.

*   *   *

Meditation, along with writing—searching, creative writing—reading, and oral communication—talking—are the mechanisms available to us for deep, meaningful dialogues that bridge historically situated cultural differences and point to linkages across sometimes nebulous frontiers. We can all use these mechanisms anywhere.

To write is to create opportunities for understanding and change. So in the classroom, a microcosm of the macrocosm, a teacher, with the help of students, *hearing* students, can invent models or strategies that will foster lifelong learning.

Writing to learn; learning to write; writing to live.

How do we use writing in a classroom, any classroom, be it geography, engineering, or mathematics? Do we assign writing at the end of a lesson for closure? To discover what one does or doesn't already know? To predict what will happen next in a text? To react or respond to a text or a discussion? How do we treat texts and ideas so that they become vital instruments for inquiry, rather than ready-made objects for students to swallow obediently and accept blindly?

Writing is the basic stuff of education. Language is the basic stuff of learning. How do we use writing—language—in our daily lives?

"What we want to say and what we feel we *can* say, given social constraints (politeness, sobriety, appropriateness, tact) demand a balancing act. We might want to blow our top, but we don't; instead we choose language to clothe our feelings in socially acceptable conventions" (Summerfield and Summerfield 1986, 11).

I was seeking creative, *enabling constraints* to somehow disable, even if momentarily, a language afflicted by "socially acceptable conventions," with the hope that students could begin to get at truths and move closer to autonomy. Students who investigate their own deeply personal experiences and establish these as a lens from which to cast a critical eye, can move from their individual positions and experiences to the more general or abstract, theorizing about the *con*texts of their lives in their culture.

So we put our desks in a circle and I sit amongst the students for introductions.

Marilynn is as white as snow, made even whiter by the dark faces surrounding her; she is a twenty-one-year-old blond Italian Irish American with a deep Brooklyn accent. She has had a tragic, complicated life for someone so young. After one year of marriage, her husband, a window washer, plummeted to his death from a skyscraper when the faulty pulleys holding his scaffold gave way. The tragedy made the city's front pages and was the lead story on the six o'clock news. Not yet over the loss of her husband, Marilynn rolled her car off the top-level entrance ramp of the Verazano Bridge onto the lower ramp when she dozed off while driving home from work in Staten Island one night.

"Theah ain't a spot on my body that ain't scarred. I spent over a yeah in the hospital. They put screws heah, theah, everywheah. I look like Frankenstein for God sake."

Anna is a young Puerto Rican American living with her husband in Staten Island. Her three-year-old daughter goes to day care or a neighbor. Anna and her husband are living the American dream. They want to own a house—"someday, you know." Both work and she, Anna, is going to school to better herself. They are making sacrifices and they work very hard, fortified by Christianity. Anna, a born-again Christian, lives and breathes the Bible.

But Marilynn and Anna landed in Remedial Writing, something they hadn't counted on; inevitably they found the system demeaning. "I thought I wrote okay. I got Bs in high school," said Marilynn. "Now theys telling me I can't write. Which is it?" Anna was more understanding, more open to her newfound condition. "I'm not good at writing. I always hated it," she admitted openly to the class. "I hate it, so I can't do it."

Marilynn and Anna were both eager to talk about themselves, as was most of the class. They already possessed the first instinct of any writer: to share. All they needed now was an object to focus on, something that had great meaning in their lives, "something that was not just an object in their environment but was treasured by virtue of its associations, its power to evoke some of their most important values" (Summerfield and Summerfield 1986, 242).

Back in 1981, Peter Elbow reflected on his "interest in the writing *process*. That is, I think I can best help you improve your writing by talking not only about the words you should end up with on paper but also about the processes that should occur on the way to that final draft" (7). Perhaps this was useful then, but I was dead certain I didn't want to talk about a prescribed *process*. *Process* evokes *a way, a method*; it's singular; the writer as one: Elbow's way touted: "the words you should end up with on paper" and "the processes that should occur on the way to that final draft." Teachers everywhere embraced it. No one blinked. Careers were made.

But I remembered what Nietzsche said about following anyone who thought "they found" truth, *a way*, an answer: run in the opposite direction.

These students, I could sense, had been given too many *ways*: do this, do that; this *way*, that *way*. And where did it get them? They're still in the same neighborhoods, still poverty stricken, still trying desperately to amend deficits—black holes—in their educations; still trying to lift themselves by their bootstraps against all odds. They've *been* in *the process*. Getting ahead means staying in place, which is synonymous with decline because, in a hierarchically arranged, capitalist culture, if one doesn't go up the vertical incline, one recedes and then loses.

I was looking at twenty-seven different faces, each with different interests, different voices, different ends in mind. Different styles and skill levels. What I needed, what I wanted was some way to enter each voice individually: how could I *hear* one student? How could I learn without *hearing*? How does one teach if the voice of a singular student, amongst all those voices, cannot be heard?

I looked around some more and found *On Writing Well* (1990), by William Zinsser, who suggested that "there are all kinds of writers and all kinds of methods, and any method that helps people to say what they want to say is the right method" (5). Valuable. That was good enough for me. But how does one tackle "any method" in the chaos of the inner-city Remedial Writing classroom? Would there be twenty-seven different "methods" for the twenty-seven different faces? What method would I deploy to stretch myself out in twenty-seven different directions? Not unlike Elbow, Zinsser is daunted by the expanse of "any method," and slides back into *process*—"The Lead," "The Ending," "Business Writing"—industrializing a very intimate, sensual evocation of one's bewilderment with the world.

Then, Lucy Calkins got my attention in *The Art of Teaching Writing* (1994), saying that "to teach well, we do not need more techniques and strategies as much as we need a vision of what is essential. It is not the number of good ideas that turn our work into art but the selection, balance, and design of those ideas" (3). I liked her language: "work into art," "vision." Yes, I was certain the students had vision. Writing, says Calkins, "begins in living with a sense of awareness," which is "an important reminder to those of us who assume that we begin to write by brainstorming ideas, listing topics, and outlining possible directions for a piece. Writing does not begin with deskwork but with lifework" (3).

So writing is moving lifework to written work, an act of transcendence, of wonderment and amazement—the art and science of seeing. Finally there was another person besides the Summerfields wondering about *the process*. Or, was it *the process* done in a different way?

I wasn't sure. But I was sure—dead certain—that my students' writings had to be real, poignant reflections of their experiences: their readings of themselves and of their culture would create art because voice from lifework is truth. As Kathleen McCormick suggests, I was aware "that it is at least in part students' lack of awareness of cultural and institutional processes that prevented them from being able to perform the apparently cognitive tasks of 'integrating their own ideas' more successfully into their essays and interpreting the text 'for a purpose of their own'" (1994, 101).

But where in education do we teach this?

Still, I was certain that my students already possessed that "awareness of cultural and institutional processes." Here I was, standing before the most oppressed, the most disenfranchised and institutionalized members of our society. In this hierarchy, I knew they could see everything; however, I also knew they were never asked about their experiences. And certainly they were never asked to bring their vital experiences into the fold of higher education—of any education at all. Their experiences were not being embraced by academe as evidence of knowledge and understanding. In essence, their experiences were rejected.

But they had—and have—something to say.

How could that young woman who was rejected by the English Department Chair and left open-mouthed as I was whisked away get remotely close to her own ideas when *the system* constantly interjects, keeping her from herself by demeaning her and rejecting her? What tools does she have to begin an inquiry into herself or others? Is she being educated for empowerment? She is being taught that there is a secret language, one that gives "allowances" or "perks" for those who know it—and she's not one, so she's being left behind. "Interpretation" becomes a foreign concept; the purpose is simply to get by, to survive, to get something—anything. Desperate, she would embrace any *process*, especially one advertising to be *the way*. Then what she learns is nothing, except how to follow—the making of a citizen, a consumer.

No, I was not looking for an assembly-line class. These Remedial Writing students at BMCC had already been processed. I wanted these students to know "how to perceive the interconnectedness of social conditions and the reading and writing practices of a culture, how to analyze those conditions and practices, and how, to some extent, to take action within and against them" (McCormick 1994, 131). At the end of the course I intended to ask them, "Knowing what you know now, how are you going to live the rest of your lives?" And I wanted the students to begin to take forceful steps toward responding to this question.

So after the class introduced themselves, I got up from my chair and began circling the students' circle from behind, round and round: no process here, only poignant prompting, constraints from which they must write in order to survive. These students understand *surviving*. They were going to *discover* their ideas, and their ideas would evolve into unique criticisms of their world(s)—and ours. They were going to re-create themselves before their very eyes.

In their nervousness, they grew silent and stopped fidgeting. It was not what I wanted that they were concerned with, it was what they, each and every one of them, wanted that made them feel uncomfortable. This is how negotiations between the private and the public take shape. These students were not being asked to follow, but rather, to listen to themselves and record what they heard.

Good tension, another condition of writing.

They were listening. I was listening.

I remembered how my parents made me think and write, whether it was after visiting the Metropolitan Museum of Art, reading a book, or having experienced a family outing to Hyde Park, New York. They'd ask questions—and I would think and write, sometimes begrudgingly, then share. During summer months, I was always made to read and write and talk: I re-created what I saw, what I experienced. I'll never forget standing before Van Gogh's *The Potato Eaters* and my mother asking, "What do you think about their faces? Now look at their hands. What's the relationship?" Poignant, acute manipulation of perspective, and from here I would evolve a theory, a sense of what I was experiencing and how I saw things: "writing does not begin with deskwork but with lifework." My life entered *The Potato Eaters* and vice versa, creating a new order of things, *lifework*, the achievement of perspective. This was a small, life-affirming act. My mother is a good teacher.

I asked students to divide their papers in half, and on the top left-hand side to write Outer, and on the top right, Inner. Then I asked them to recollect an incident that had affected them deeply and changed, even slightly, what they thought, what they may believe in, or how they now think about certain things.

I wanted students to recall an incident so powerful as to have affected their perspectives. I wanted them to reenter their experiences (Outer) and to find a basis for their own ideas by closely examining their emotions (Inner).

I gave them twenty-five to thirty minutes for each writing, the Outer and the Inner. And they wouldn't have to read these aloud: safety and honesty.

Marilynn's Writing:

Outer

My eight grade graduation the only one who wanted to go was my mother. My father said its not important that if my sisters didn't win any awards he knew for sure I wasn't going to. He was on vacation and couldn't come home. The afternoon was beautiful the sun high but not hot I had my mother watching. My name was called three times for achievement awards. When we arrived at home the family was very surprised they couldn't believe I did it. I felt I proved them all wrong. My high school graduation came my father couldn't make it again he had a very important golf game to go to. That he didn't need to be there my mother would go. Everyone was allowed only 4 tickets and they all wanted more and all I could fill up was one chair. I gave the extra tickets to my friend who her entire family wanted to be there that day. My mother sat in the audience smiled and took pictures as if only me and her existed in the world and I accomplished something she never saw before but in fact I did the same thing I did four years prior. I didn't know I did it again myself. My father told

Inner

I've failed before I knew I did or didn't. I never thought I was smart enough or could do anything right. I never thought it could happen to me and when it did I thought someone made a mistake. I was very proud of myself and thought there was some hope for me if I could only find it or talk about it. I talked and was told I could be whatever I wanted to be but I couldn't believe it. I always thought I'd be a nothing never go anywhere. Not be important. I was scared of the future so I prayed it would disappear and I'd be old and finished living. I had a lot of regret because I couldn't believe in myself and make something of myself. I couldn't please others so nothing could be worth it I wanted to just give up. If I tried and failed everyone would laugh. I believe in my future. And that I could make a difference in someone's life and if anyone feels like I've felt I'd like to tell them so they don't think they're the only one like I did for so long. This is my strength to carry on and succeed for myself and it feels special I have self-esteem.

me that night that I couldn't go to college and I wasn't smart enough to do it and it would be wasting time and money also because he didn't have the money he was paying for my other sisters. I was being lazy and was thinking school would be easier than work. I never worked because he didn't allow it our studies were suppose to be more important. I didn't know what to do.

Anna's Writing:

Outer

I had an argument with my soon to be daughters God Mother. One day It was late about 2:30pm in the morning. I was locked out, because I lost my keys on my way home. I think I lost them in the cab that I had taken home. I did not notice that I had lost my keys Until I had started looking for them. Since, I could not find them, I rang the door bell. Lamont did not answer the door. I thought what am I going to do. He is not home. After 10 minutes sitting in front of the house, it had started to poor. The night was cold. Now I was cold and wet and locked out. Since, I lived in a two family house I rang Sharron the lady who lived above me. Sharron was kind enough to allow me to use her phone. The first thing I did was call my house just in incase he picked up the phone. That's when I decided to call Maria. I thought for sure she would let me spend the night in her house when she picked up the phone

Inner

I was feeling angry hurt and shocked. I was also confused I did not understand why she had responded to me in that manner. She was going to be my daughter's god mother. Maybe she really did not care for Maegan, or myself. Well after that, I felt like I hated her. She was not going to be Maegan's God mother after that. I am a born again Christian, and knew that I should not hold a grudge with anyone. Well I have been going to Church and studing the bible and came across a verse that said: "If you have a fight with someone you should forgive them the way you want the Lord to forgive you." The same day that I ran into that verse I bumped into Maria. I did not want to say hi, but I felt that the lord was testing me. So I obeyed and said hi. That was very hard and I hated to do it. We talked for a few minutes and we went on our way. It is now September 24th, 1994, calling my house I still see her and talk to

I said, "Hi Maria." She said what are you doing at this time? I went on to explain how it was an emergency and was locked out and had no where to stay. I also told her on my way home I has lost my keys and Lamont was not home. Her response was. No you may not spend the night in my house, and thats to bad next time be more responsible and hung up on me right away. I was so hurt and shocked. Well, Sharron felt really bad for me so she allowed me to spend the night in her house. I was so thankful, because I was in a warm house. She started to make up the sofa for me and made me some tea. Lamont finally go in about 3:30am. The first thing I did was ask him where he had been. He said he was in Frank & Claudia. I wish I would have thought of calling their house. After I got in I told him all about the encounter, I had with Maria. He was appalled at the way she had treated me. Well, after that I wanted nothing to do with Maria.

her. Although we will never be close I try to maintain an ameable relationship with her.

Representative of the class, Marilynn and Anna revisited incidents that confused their preconceived notions concerning the roles people are given to play in our culture. They are beginning to read themselves and their culture. Their Inner, private selves are colliding with an Outer, public morality, bifurcating a voice each believed to be whole, complete. Now these new, apparently disparate voices are demanding to be heard. Not yet in confluence, the identity of each young woman—who they are today—is being compromised, even aggressively questioned, by the institutions of family, education, and religion. To compromise, here, means to lose something—something big. We can note their apprehensions in their grammar; it is tenuous, strained. Yet they are primarily concerned with speaking and getting out their ideas. They can't help themselves; they can't keep quiet. They are courageous. Marilynn grows increasingly mistrustful and confused about her potential and abilities; Anna, challenged by the actions of a "friend," feels alone and senses her inadequacy in the face of Christianity.

Their grammar suggests that negotiating the rest of their lives is going to be daunting, that their visions are once again being challenged by the formulations of governing institutions. However, along with the stress comes the "newness" of being able to (re)-create themselves within this usually foreboding structure. Education is opening doors, not closing them, as they are accustomed. It's a different, unfamiliar, and perhaps productive stress.

Marilynn and Anna are wondering about what possibilities are open to them, about whether they will be able to develop their own individualities and hence be productive for both themselves and the rest of society. This is the obvious tension between their Inner and Outer worlds: experiences and deeply felt emotions and desires are colliding with perceptions about their outside worlds. Excellent tension for writing.

Marilynn and Anna are trying to make sense of themselves; they are reading their lives within the *con*texts of the culture that has given them the methods by which to exist: they are trying to *do the right thing*. Marilynn and Anna are recognizing that disagreements exist, so they are reluctant to plunge into relativism. Both writers are tentative; however, here is where possibilities for further development exist. Excellent tension for learning. Here is where their grammar will begin to conform.

> Tentativeness implies that meaning is not derived solely from the text, but rather is produced as a result of a complex interaction of cognitive and cultural, as well as textual, variables, any or all of which could possibly become the subject of analysis in a later draft. A tentative, open approach that stresses issues and questions rather than mere statements of "facts" further allows students to develop, and possibly even change, their position on the subject about which they are writing *during the course of their writing*. A tentative, as opposed to a closed approach, leaves interpretive options open and regards writing as an occasion for discovery rather than a tool for recording what is already known. (McCormick 1994, 112–113)

Where do we go from here?

Oh my God, what's all this? Students are wondering. *Where did all of this come from? Look at all these mistakes. This is a mistake, right?*

We write some more.

Marilynn and Anna are tightly wound in the constraints that they have incited, so we loosen this up just a bit and take one giant step back to *enable* the beginning stages of reflection. I ask that they reflect on writing only: what do you notice about writing? what do you notice about your own writing? what can you say about your writing?

Marilynn's Reflection:

My writing looks good to me but not to anyone else. My words get jumbled up. I can't stay focused or get the most important thought across and if do I keep repeating it. I stumble on thoughts. I have great thoughts and when I get a pen and paper my mind goes blank as if the thoughts were never there!

Anna's Reflection:

Writing helps me see what Im thinking about. But sometimes I see that all my thinking is running together. Running on sentences they call it I think. Nevertheless I got everything down I was thinking. This kind of writing is good. But I need to work on spelling and grammar.

Marilynn and Anna are very hard on themselves. They've learned this pattern; however, the Reflection serves to open the writer up to her own sense of the craft she is tackling for the first time in a creative way. The writer needs to see herself exploring in order to find the right notes, hit the right keys. This is arduous work, but we can see from Marilynn and Anna that it's already paying off. The teacher, too, is involved, learning to *see and hear* what her students yearn: *I stumble on thoughts . . . I need to work on spelling and grammar* cannot be dismissed, but addressed coherently and effectively *within* the context of their work, their worlds.

My own mother's sense about how to coerce me into a conversation about perspective—"What do you think about their faces? Now look at their hands. What's the relationship?"—compelled me to ask the students to reread their Inner and Outer writings with a critical eye: step back, look at the writing as if it's not yours, in awe, wonderment; look inside, way inside, and tell me what you see and make a list of ideas that reside within the writing.

"You mean read between the lines, Professor Vila?"

Read between the lines and make a list, one idea following the next.

We are entering the science of writing and grammar; we are realizing intention versus purpose; we are, in effect, closing in on significa-tion, but the trick is to never quite get there.

Marilynn's List	Anna's List
Self-esteem	Friendship
Fear	Faith
Love	Christianity
Faith	
Father	

Then we performed a thirty-second exercise that asks that students stare at their words and observe themselves in the task: to what word or words do your eyes always return? Try to move your eyes away from this word or words. Do they keep coming back? Rewrite this word, or words on a blank sheet of paper.

Marilynn wrote *Fear* and *Father*, of course; Anna wrote *Christianity*, nothing else, showing how overwhelming the concept may really be for her.

Then fifteen-minutes of freewriting on these words: what are you thinking? what does your *lifework* tell you? I am wondering.

Marilynn's:

> Why does he say and do the things he does. Doesn't he know everyone isn't perfect and isn't always going to shine. He should be very supportive a helping hand loving, caring, nurishing, approving. A guide to lead you to the future and be all you can be not what they need or want you to be.
>
> I don't want anyone to put me down only tell me I could do better there is no failure only room for approval, not being able to finish what I start, so I make sure I always do no matter what. My fear of failure made me stay away from a lot of things in my life people/friends maybe this is why I can't trust. Will it carry into my future.
>
> I'm trying not to let it but it does sometimes come out of people I know and sometimes think I love. So I tell them immediately so they can try not to do it again and if they do I cut them off. I don't need it anymore. I do fear the most of being alone and that nobody will ever approve of what I do. Complex.

Anna's:

> It's very hard to be a Christian. Since I became born again I notice how much God challenges me. With Maria I knew I had to be better than I was behaving because I had to "turn the other cheeck". But somehow I can't forgive her all the way, though I know God wants me to. I just can't. Maria did something very wrong. I was a friend in need and she turned me away.
>
> This happened many times to Christ but he turned the situation around by putting himself in the other persons place. Christianity means tolerance which is the hardest thing for us to do. We are not perfect. Christianity I think realizes this. This is why they have rules we have to live by. Sometimes it's hard but it's the trying that counts. I know I'll make mistakes but isn't that why Christ fell when he carried the cross means?

Already, Marilynn and Anna have entered into their subject and are beginning to gain critical distance; they are examining what their experiences mean, and they are extrapolating. "He should be supportive," Marilynn is saying about her father as if she is writing a moral *how-to* text. Anna, on the other hand, is more philosophical, and critical: "Christianity means tolerance which is the hardest thing for us to do." Both Marilynn and Anna are closer to the tone characteristic of a college essay; they are moving slowly, from deeply felt emotions motivated by dramatic conditions to a seemingly more objective, or more *removed* and therefore critical, form. This is evident in their decision to paragraph, even during a freewriting exercise! And it is obvious in their grammar: they know that they are composing in a different tone; it rearticulates their grammar, and I've yet to say a word on the subject. This is natural to both writers—to all writers, I propose.

Students are doing this on their own, devising their own processes to work through the enabling constraints I am voicing. I have yet to see any of their work and 2 seventy-five-minute classes have elapsed: it's their sign of ownership. Their writings are transcending their experiences and redefining their identities in new ways. The students have created subjects of themselves and are listening to their own music. They are involved in negotiations that will try to explain the contradictions they are noticing, rather than explaining them away. "Even texts that appear coherent," argues McCormick, following Barthes, "can often be regarded as sites of struggle, as semiotic battlefields in which diverse and often contradictory meanings compete for dominance" (1994, 126). *This* is learning, and the students amidst their struggles have yet to come to the literature—more semiotic battlefields I have waiting in the wings—and their final essays.

Now I ask them to take a leap: Imagine yourselves in front of one hundred people, an audience, and you're standing alone on a stage; you have to speak to these people about the work you have before you. How would you go about it? Where would you begin? How would you say it? How would you make it lively? Use everything you've already done to put this "thing" together, but remember, if you don't entertain and interest your audience, they'll leave. You must voice your ideas powerfully. This is about achieving power.

This is a grammar exercise, as well as an exercise meant to expose problems with transitions. A writing teacher's job is to expose writing problems, not conceal them, or sweep them under the rug with hyperbole.

Marilynn:

We all carry unsolved feelings around with us. Many things happen in our life that effect us life long. They all can be resolved if we focus on our main issues.

Many complexes are built or our self esteem is torn apart from simple words said. We should all be aware of our tone and sensitivity of the person we're speaking to.

When someone looks up to you you should have as much confidence in them as they do for you.

When you're given a title in this world you should stand up to that title or don't take it at all.

When I was told by my father that I couldn't make it or it was too difficult for me I believed it and gave up why not he did on me before he even knew.

A "Father" is a title a lot of men take on and don't take the responsibilities such as being supportive not financially but emotionally. It's a title that you need to be a guide for someones future. If you didn't get to do something in your life don't condem someone one want to do or try.

This is not only for a father it can be for a mother or anyone if someone is confiding in you. You should be able to give all you can give and if you can't explain why then don't let someone think otherwise.

How can we resolve our problems is to search within ourselves for strength. We need to put our strengths to reality and push forward.

If you look at yourself as a failure you will be a failure. Don't fear what other fear. Do what you need to do to succeed.

We all need love, nourishment, encouragement, approval, and faith we usually have a guide but if not find it within ourself.

The initial four paragraphs are extremely interesting. Marilynn takes on a voice meant to passionately and assuredly state ideas: "We all carry unsolved feelings around with us." Efficient, but then she realizes that she must begin to strike a chord, to narrow *and* maintain tonal quality, strength: "They all can be resolved if we focus on our main issues." It's coming from her, only. She has done this naturally, without coercion or direct guidance, but by remembering that there is an audience: performance strikes for her the proper anxiety. Then in the subsequent three paragraphs, Marilynn builds three theories: there is a relationship between "complexes" and "our self esteem"; being responsible to those that "look up to you"; and a "title" must be worn with dignity. The first four paragraphs therefore establish a circle of ideas, a rhetoric of influences.

This is classic. Marilynn could be in Athens, rather than Tribeca — or are they one and the same?

The answer is, in Marilynn's paragraphing strategy. She understands that the ideas in the initial paragraphs are very significant and will need *space* of their own to air. This is a rhetorical convention equated with traditional texts, as well as a device paradoxically linked to power management, and both of these are legacies from the Greek rhetorical tradition. She is structuring her ideas classically because she has *read* enough of her culture to already understand how to *arrange* her negotiations; however, she is still tentative about where to go, how to develop: the main concern during the beginning prompts to the assignment, here, turning up as problems with transition and critical thinking, we would say. But she really does not illustrate *classic* composition problems with orthodox rules and regulations of composition, as some—those that placed her in remediation—might have it; she is instead demonstrating an abiding allegiance to herself as subject, to her culture's domination and to her deep need to create an identity for herself. Her writing is already a searching, a way to try to understand the woman she has become, and will become.

Writing, then, as illustrated by Marilynn, is the study of the art and science of transcendence through language. She's going to prove this. Thus like a Greek, Marilynn takes for granted her text's *function* and its *manifestation*.

Is there a text in the class?

Yes, Marilynn's.

But in what *context*(s)?

"It is only when students begin to see that their subjectivities are part of a larger cultural framework," says McCormick, "that they can develop the skills necessary to evaluate critically the particular positions they take up" (1994, 171).

Marilynn's Reflection on the above writing:

I have a lot of unsolved feelings I need to resolve them not to carry them on into my future and take them out one someone I do care for. As much as I want to succeed I don't want to hurt anyone or step on anyone while doing it.

I need to be supportive of myself and others. Not to fear but to live and let live. Leave mental goals for myself.

Then she wrote some notes a few lines beyond her reflection.

strength: logic/resolved (method question)
weakness: too general (preaching: show and tell, instead)
clarify and simplified: how to find one (guide)
how to do it!
How does one: (1)focus in an age of confusion? (2)How does one realize a main issue when to be human means we have many?

And then she writes: "Sometimes we are too young and confused to know our troubles."

Marilynn then discussed with me what she had written. We spoke about where she might like to go with this. She went to classmates during one of our workshop days and asked similar questions of them.

Then I warned her, and everyone else: You're going to read something about Socrates.

She wrote in her notebook: "Socrates." And asked for dates, writing: "469–399 B.C." I felt the need to give her, and the rest of the class, a couple of words to look up in the dictionary: *didactic* and *rhetoric*.

Marilynn's Next Draft, before Reading "The Crito":

Unresolved feelings are carried through life. Many things happened in life that affect a person forever. They all can be resolved if we focus on our issues.

Youth keeps people from really understanding troubles. Conversations should be at the level of intelligence of the person you're speaking to.

People communicate with someone they look up to and believe in. Tone and actions are very important in interpretation. This way no complexes are built in and self esteem torn apart.

For instance, on my 8th grade graduation my father told me that I wouldn't be accomedated so it wasn't important to be there; then when high school finished he told me that college was too difficult for me, I believed it and gave up.

Titles are given in this world so people have and can get guidance and support. Support not of a financial matter but emotional.

Searching within ourselves by evaluating what each of us learned is a means to understand ourselves and overcome dilemmas. Going back to situations and putting our experiences into order with our new learned knowledge.

Everyone needs love, nurishment, encouragement, approval and faith; so if you're guiding someone don't knock them, understand them.

Marilynn's piece, while developing, is still aphoristic, relying on her understanding of how to get her point across through terse formulations. Her perplexity is characterized by her intense desire to be critical and penetrating, yet powerful, even dogmatic, for emphasis. Marilynn is dealing with a high-level problem of composition, a critical problem—a philosophical problem swarming the late stages of the twentieth century, as Jacques Derrida informs us: "From one discourse to another, the difference lies only in the mode of inhabiting the interior of a conceptuality destined, or already submitted, to decay" (1976, 85). The Greeks, for instance, called for an ideal of public speaking that was verbal, expositional, discrete, and hierarchical; however, our popular culture has taken this and made it *function* as advertisement, and some argue that this is another sign of decay.

Thus Marilynn's bind: the intense labor required to break from the grips of popular culture's fixation on the mundane and banal, through its replication of ancient devices now bastardized, and the critical need to involve herself in a meaningful examination of herself among others. Marilynn's bind defines the role of the teacher, especially for those

of us who labor with composition: an individual who provides meaningful *enabling constraints*, which compel students to write, experiment,
and imagine their roles and their futures based on their critical assess-
ments of our culture.

Marilynn is ready for literature. I handed the class the *Crito*. They
gasped, yet smiled tentatively: this is what college is supposed to be
about.

"You think we can read this?" the class exclaimed, sounding much
like teachers who ask, "You think they can read this?" then answer,
"No, they can't read this. They're remedial writers."

They *can read this*, I say to colleagues.

You've already read this, I said to the class.

"This is really old. How will we understand it?"

You already do, I said. Each of you will see what you already see,
what you already know and have put forth. Read what you know, then
we'll talk and fill in the blanks. You know it.

> What is writing? How can it be identified? What certitude of essence
> must guide the empirical investigation? Guide it in principle, for it is
> a necessary fact that empirical investigation quickly activates reflex-
> ion upon essence. It must operate through "examples," and it can
> be shown how this impossibility of beginning at the beginning of the
> straight line, as it is assigned by the logic of transcendental reflexion,
> refers to the originality (under erasure) of the trace, to the root of
> writing. What the thought of the trace has already taught us is that
> it could not be simply submitted to the onto-phenomenological ques-
> tion of essence. The trace *is nothing*, it is not an entity, it exceeds the
> question *What is?* and contigently makes it possible. (Derrida 1976, 75)

I was looking for their readings of *the trace*—for them to understand
a trace and its relation to their points of view, their lives—believing that
since popular culture was inhabited by it and vice versa, and had done
its best to obfuscate and erase it, then Marilynn, and the rest of the
class, would certainly be able *to read* themselves in the *Crito*. And hopefully, I trusted, they could experience how the *Crito read them*.

As McCormick suggests, "By recognizing that all forms of reading
constitute interventions into contemporary debates, students can begin
to learn ways of adjudicating among them and ways of determining
how to develop a position of their own with critical awareness and conviction" (1994, 171–172).

What does this mean for the teacher? Ruth Vinz suggests

> Teachers shift their attention from particular texts to experiences that
> help readers affect meanings that are multiple and dynamic. What
> readers bring to their readings, the feeling or associations evoked, the
> contested interpretations leading to critical readings, all and each

promise a fruitful means for producing more self-aware and socially aware meanings from literary texts. These directions aren't part of the repertoire of principles or practices for many literature teachers, but for those who are influenced by the theories, there is an entirely different set of notions about texts, readers, and teachers as well as about structures and experiences enacted in practice. (1996, 169)

The class went off to read the *Crito*. Typically they saw the things they had already written about. Then each student contributed something different, during two class discussions that involved intense conversation, with me writing their *critical* ideas on the board. Through this *collaborative knowledge*, as I call it, the entire text became clear and, most important, nonthreatening and *functional*. They taught themselves. I, in turn, prodded and nurtured, adding historical points: where Greece is; what Greece was; who Socrates was; who Plato and Aristotle were; Greece's relationship to Egypt; Greece's relationship to Rome, and so forth.

The students would tell me of Greece's relationship to us.

After working through some collaborative grammar and editing strategies—namely, studying the basic structure of a sentence and analyzing the functions of verbs, which I promoted as critical for a concise sentence—and by understanding that *revision* is a reformulation of ideas, a revisiting with another consciousness, the students went off to their drafts to try to put everything together.

Marilynn's final draft, complete with title:

Words Are Precious

Unresolved feelings are carried through life. Many things happen in life that affect a person forever. All problems can be resolved by focusing on issues.

For instance, youth keeps people from really understanding troubles. This is because of a lack of knowledge. Conversations should be at the level of intelligence of the person you're speaking to. For example, in "The Crito," a dialogue of Plato, Socrates spoke to Criton before he was put to death. Socrates spoke to Criton in a way he could understand Socrates' point of view and what he was doing and why, at a level which Criton could comprehend (447–459).

Another example, opposite from "The Crito," my father told me that I wouldn't be accommodated at my eight grade graduation so it wasn't important to be there; the same situation happened when I graduated high school. He told me that college was too expensive and too difficult for me. I was crushed. I believed it and gave up.

When speaking to people it is important to think before. Tones and actions are very important for interpretation, especially to whom you are speaking with. Then complexes won't be built and self esteem torn apart.

Everyone needs love, encouragement, and approval. When guiding someone, such as when Socrates spoke there was an understanding for what was said. The points of view were known, where they came from and where they would continue to grow to (447–459).

People choose who they want to communicate with. It is usually a person they look up to and have confidence in. In "The Crito," Socrates said, "that of the opinions which people hold, we ought to value some highly, but not all 'because' the good ones are those of the wise, the bad ones those of the foolish?"(451)

In this world titles are given which a person should stand up to it or don't take it at all. Title such as father and mother are given so people have and can get guidance and support. Support is not of a financial matter but emotional.

For example, in The "Crito," Socrates stated a man practicing athletics should not fear those who blame and have opinions but only listen to the expert who will oversee his training and he will not suffer any harm (451).

To overcome our dilemmas of everyday life searching within ourselves by going back and evaluating situations and putting our experiences in order with our learned knowledge can let us understand and grow into healthier minded individuals.

Something has happened to Marilynn's writing. Still not totally free from aphorisms, her tone has mellowed and is more philosophical; she has slid into the persona of the intellectual, the critical thinker, and she's using her experiences and a text to refabricate herself and her understandings. In her writing portfolio letter, Marilynn asserts, "My vision into writing has gone from the personal to the more objective . . . I know I have more to learn and I am willing. I now know that I am able . . . I chose these particular writings . . . because they all contain sentimental parts of my life that are dear to me. Every situation gave me the strength and courage to carry me through to today. I made it this far, I know that I can go further."

Marilynn can see this, *read* these assertions in her writing: she feels this, knows this to be truth. Socrates is now a "sentimental part" of her life too. Marilynn is not a basic writer, though she was placed there through standardized testing; she is, however, an individual who has been damaged, by family, by institutions—by relationships. There is indeed a difference if we change our perception of students, disallowing remediation as a feeding frenzy for those who seek to separate rather than join together.

Those who seek standardization for all, even though students clearly demonstrate their vast differences, use superficial grammatical problems like weapons for teachers to demean and oppress, driving Marilynn and others like her further to the margins. This is what makes teaching difficult or impossible at times: ours is a job of undoing the damage our education system and other systems have done, so that students can rediscover their losses. Marilynn says, "my accomplishments have been noticed by others." This is why they come to school: to recognize themselves *in* other's readings of them—to be noticed.

It is the will moving toward power, *a will to power*.

Only writing can do this. Why do we pretend otherwise even in the face of our own educations, which prove this to be true? Way do we read Shakespeare? Milton? Morrison? Anyone, for that matter? In the act of reading (someone's writing), we become acquainted with ourselves and our power; and in the act of writing, we experience ourselves experiencing the world around us: we can see ourselves.

Writing *is* power.

Anna's final draft of the same assignment

Laws We Must Live By

Christianity is a religion derived from the teachings of Jesus Christ. Jesus was a Jewish man born in Jerusalem almost two thousand years ago. *The Bible* states, "he is the son of God." According to the *American Heritage* dictionary God is: a being conceived as the perfect, omnipotent, omniscient originator and ruler of the universe, the principal object of faith and worship in monotheistic religions. His teachings consist of the Ten Commandments. They are laws he want us to live by (Exodus 20–1).

The Bible is a book written by man under the direction of God. *The Bible* is interpreted many different ways. For example, the Jewish believe Jesus Christ is a messenger and not the son of God. Christians believe Jesus is the son of God. Because of interpretations we now have different religions.

The Bible teaches me how to be a Christian and explains how anger is not part of Christianity. Although aware of this, I could not help feeling angry and resentful towards Maria. Maria was a dear friend of mine. She was someone I could count on. Because our relationship I decided she would be Maegan's God mother. Soon after my decision, I saw a side of Maria that was selfish and mean. I needed her in an emergency and she flatly refused me. Maria told me she did not want to be bothered and would appreciate it if I left her alone. After that incident our relationship would have ceased, but since I'm a Christian and with God's help I was able to forgive her.

As I read *The Bible* I came across a verse that said, "So if you are standing before the alter in the temple offering a sacrifice to God, and suddenly remember that a friend has something against you, leave your sacrifice there beside the alter and go and apologize and be reconciled to him, and then come offer your sacrifice to God" (Matthew 5:23–24). After reading this I knew I had obeyed God's word when I forgave Maria.

Through my readings I've discovered that men like Socrates had to endure similar circumstances. In "The Crito," Socrates is in jail and facing death, his final punishment. Criton his dear friend, tries to convince him to escape; he warns him if they plan to escape they must do it under the blanket of night.

Socrates willingly makes his decision to deal with the consequences no matter the cost. He accepts death before banishment. Socrates tries to explain to Criton how important it is to abide by the laws that are established for order. If he does not endure his punishment he is setting the wrong example for society (459).

In her portfolio letter, Anna says that she found this, and other assignments "challenging because I had to combine research work with my own ideas and experience . . . I felt I was incapable of handling such a project." Anna's reflection is beginning to distort the strangulation inflicted on her by education's demands that she conform to a hierarchical order—a disorienting scheme meant to indoctrinate her into a citizenship of conformity, silence, and consumerism. She goes on to say that she is "able to freewrite with confidence and assuredness, qualities I did not possess at the beginning of the semester . . . This accomplishment has brought me to a new place in my writing. It has instilled confidence, something that is necessary to become a good writer."

Both Anna and Marilynn have entered new areas in their writing; they recognize where they have been and they see themselves within their culture. Anna and Marilynn are using words like *vision*, *courage*, and *strength* to describe their activities; they understand how difficult it is to be *objective*, what a *challenge* it is, and they are realistic and content with their *accomplishments*. Ultimately, they notice, with confidence *and* assuredness, how *free* they have become. This is essential for anyone desiring an identity that is whole. This is essential for anyone wanting to be a *good writer*—a learner.

Thus, Job's "sea monsters" speak out, entering academe's "secret language." They need not be watched, but rather, coaxed and encouraged. Or because they are beginning to awaken from 'the dreams' that scare them, will we watch them ever more closely? Writing, reading, and dialogue make the system more understandable. The difficult task of navigating through the system's language configurations is being learned. These students already have *wisdom*; they are learning to recover trust in themselves.

The writings of Anna and Marilynn are concerned with notions of change, which a creatively structured writing portfolio promotes. Texts, literary or otherwise, become fertilizer rather than scarecrows meant to keep students away from budding knowledge. Concomitant, varied writing samples afford students the potential for *re*-presenting different voices and different outlooks and allow students to assess themselves as they read their world; in turn, teachers read students reading us and their world, creating rich terrain for honest evaluation—of students, teachers, and education as a whole. Which is only proper.

But tragically, this is no panacea. Let's not be fooled. "We always live at the time we live and not at some other time," says John Dewey in *Experience and Education* (1938), "and only by extracting at each present time the full meaning of each present experience are we prepared for doing the same thing in the future. This is the only preparation which in the long run amounts to anything" (51).

While the *enabling constraints* proved so fruitful for Anna, Marilynn, and others, I *lost* four students in a class of twenty-seven. By *lost* I mean they did not pass the WAT, *the system's* measure, and their portfolios, though they did show improvement, were not indicative of the growth experienced by others. Their growth was deemed insufficient by the culture of the system, of which I am a part.

I don't know what to do about this—yet. I'm looking and searching, knowing that these four students do have visions and ideas they want to express so as to enable a *new*, perhaps different identity to emerge. These four students are still very much immersed in a will to power, a will to achieve a significant sense of self, which they are more than willing to express; however, they need more time. But time is money in our culture, and taking too much time means a bottom-line loss. Nevertheless, it is obvious these students require more time to feel their way around, ingest the stimuli, and synthesize. Perhaps they learn differently and I had no time to assess their methods. Perhaps they have not rid themselves of the mechanisms of oppression, have not yet fully grasped the mechanisms of freedom: full use of the imagination. These four *lost* students are neither here nor there, so they are nowhere, still burdened by our culturally defined remnants of devastation and wallowing in a "middle-world," a nondescript world characterized as bad, or ugly, bleak, or dark—a *minority's* world of nonachievers, we say.

In *The Survival of Domination* (1978), Barry Adam tells us that "oppression which is imminent in everyday life and necessitates immediate and repeated responses, builds a repertoire of habits and attitudes among its victims. Behavior that is mundane, routine, and taken for granted tends to escape the notice of the more dramatic macrohistories" (1–2). These students need more than writing. In the meantime, and dramatically, we punish them even more by pushing them further out and away from any semblance of a learning environment because they are poignant reminders of what *we* have done, and are still doing to them. Then we learn how not to *see*, nor how to *hear*:

> Socially structured life constraints elicit behavior which adjusts, accommodates, or subordinates itself to adverse situations in the interest

of survival and thereby functions to reproduce the constraining order. Much of everyday life cannot but submit to the *rationality* of given social order. (2)

So we become complacent with the status quo. Or we *un*-rationalize the given social order and learn to walk down other avenues, created with imagination and insight, knowing full well that this *different* or *new* road will meet with great resistance. But how are we to *profit* without resistance?

Note

1. In 1996, 91,000 New York City school children did not have desks to begin their scholastic year; they did not even have learning environments. At this same time, we were involved in a national election whereby the main topics of discussion were the perverse behavior of political advisors, gay marriages, and abortion, but no one spoke about these students who did not have a place to learn. As these 91,000 students went to their bathrooms and hallways and stairwells to learn, one wonders where the liberal left is? Where the moderates are? The conservatives? One even wonders why teachers report to their respective schools rather than striking and shutting down the entire city of New York? Why is it that 91,000 children without learning environments is not a national tragedy? Why is it that the futures of 91,000 dispossessed New York City school children is not of primary concern in a national election? A year later, the situation worsened, though now it is camouflaged behind urges for the "new education technologies" which will purportedly solve our nightmares; however, students still report to bathrooms and hallways for their learning while New York City's Mayor Rudolph Giuliani has made the issue of jaywalkers dominant in local politics.

Chapter Five

Up from Mean Streets: Realism and Learning in a Renaissance Age

"Everyone's life is influenced by institutions in some way . . . It seems that we are free to choose our way of life, but in reality we have to obey the rules dictated by institutions." So writes Anton, a young Russian immigrant in a Remedial Writing class at Borough of Manhattan Community College. This Russian student sees something of his old world in his new one: or are these worlds one and the same?

"Abraham Rodriguez, Jr., in his story "The Boy Without a Flag," shows what disobedience of the rules may lead to," the Russian student continues to write introspectively and critically. "The author says: '*You do as you're told if you do not want big trouble.*' To survive in our society these days, we have to make certain sacrifices. Many times, we have to go on compromises. We often have to deny ideals so that we can live in peace with institutions."

To *live in peace with institutions* is to repress our idealism, says Anton; it is the dictum for compromise and discipline imposed by the bastions of social *order*ing we've created to keep us in check. Anton has learned this quite well; his constraint-based knowledge, the way our culture presently operates, the way it represents, is inculcated in his being.

We can use these compromises, or forms of discipline, to contextualize reading and writing experiences and to learn, that is, for wisdom. Students can *re*-order themselves along lines that might begin to impose impressions of *their* world—ownership—onto institutions. In other words, Anton's voice can be heard. But there are questions. Will it be heard and felt—by us? What imprint will it leave? Can we teachers effectively re-create ourselves, and our worlds of mass markets and media's attempts to homogenize collective experiences by appealing to the lowest common denominator?

Can we as a society provide for students the creative, exciting learning environments required for poignant, critical insights like Anton's? I believe we must: we have no other choice.

But what *is* learning? How do we account for it? How can we begin to define it in our technocratic globalization of experiences so as to enable educational environments that are more *realistic*, more in touch with who we are and what we're involved with as we lurch past the millennium? Along with so many other changes we're undergoing in our culture today, does it not make sense that *learning*, too, is metamorphosing? Given the prevalence of TV, electronic gaming, and film in our students' lives, of videos, CDs, different text designs, word processing, hypertexts, electronic imaging, and the digitizing of classrooms—isn't the way we now *learn* quite different than, say, ten years ago?

Are we working, along with Howard Gardner in *Frames of Mind* (1993), "to take into account the various differences in individual profiles of intelligences within an educational setting," taking the care and the time to describe "an 'individual-centered school'" (xv)?

The challenge is to create a learning environment whereby a full range of symbol systems—music, bodily, spatial, personal, linguistic, and logical and numerical—are not only taken into account for assessment purposes, but are a complete and integrated part of the curriculum. Students must be allowed to devise their own methods for expressing themselves and, thus, for learning; they must be encouraged to find their interests, and their visions (12–30).

Our learning environments have changed, and in some instances worsened; likewise, our students are quite different. Whether they are American-born or not, they come into our classrooms from worldly experiences, even cyber-worldly experiences—sometimes too worldly. We must recognize this reality, and use it!

Anton is a Russian student and a burgeoning American voice; he's representative of all of our students, perhaps all of us, struggling to find ways to remain true to moral principles—to vision—while negotiating an existence in a public sphere he never assumed would be *so* hostile, especially in his *new* American world of such vast promise. There is a tone in Anton of a romanticism gone sour, a condition most Americans are experiencing, though we can't seem to put our fingers on our disease during this time of momentous transition, and so grow anxious about where we're headed and what we will become. Like Anna and Marilynn, Anton is caught up in a conflict between his inner self as it collides or conflates—or both—with an outer reality; it is the private versus the public, again.

"The meaning of the word FREEDOM [*his caps*] is lost in the pile of norms dictated by institutions," says Anton in a critical reading of Abraham Rodriguez's short story, "The Boy Without a Flag," a creative and profound inquiry into freedom and individual rights as experienced by a Puerto Rican American boy attempting to define himself, though he's lodged between two cultures: a newer, foreboding, and unforgiving American culture, and an older, fading Puerto Rican culture.

Anton fully comprehends and is able to identify in the Rodriguez short story—that knowledge *succeeds* the paths by which power advances and that knowledge will therefore acquire new objects of study along the lines on which power is exercised. Anton echos, much as Michel Foucault, who argues in *Discipline & Punish* (1979) that this is the way power behaves in our society, how it is used, even nourished. Anton has experienced this, he's living through it.

Anton's understanding stems from his "practical" experience determined by his position in two cultures: first, a marginalized Russian, then a Russian immigrant marginalized in this new American culture. Anton is experiencing the machinations of power—as the marginalized usually do; he's expressing a philosophy based on *his* synthesis of the Rodriguez text and *his* constraint-based knowledge.

With Anton, we are in the presence of an emerging "organic intellectual," Gramsci's notion and a poignant characteristic of the Renaissance Thinker *in* a Renaissance Age. Gramsci believes that out of the "lower classes" will emerge intellectuals that have gained *new, different* and even *provocative* wisdom because they bring with them the experiences and upbringing of their class designation while at the same time having appropriated the knowledge and the language of the higher order of a given society, the class that designates meaning and creates the means of exchange. This "organic intellectual," who will mold both sides of the equation into a fresh critique of the culture, grows and thus integrates "the ways" of the higher class with the experiences of the lower class, his/her cultural roots. In other words, the "organic intellectual" emerges as a hybrid, an individual who will inform us because s/he brings to the public sphere, both personal experiences as a marginalized individual, as well as experiences gathered from a sojourn in the halls of privilege. The "organic intellectual" offers a new and fresh perspective. Anton, by his own admission, is of poor, Russian background, and is here in the United States to gain a higher education; though it is at BMCC, he is, nevertheless, learning to manipulate and negotiate the language of power, the "cash language," as Jesse Jackson defines it.

Learning, we can therefore begin to articulate, involves the confidence *and* courage to speak one's self to the world, symbolically, regardless of the consequences. This is individual *efficacy*; it is personal and, even in the most supportive of environments, it takes a very long time to evolve. To notice and understand this aspect of learning, accountability and assessment have to be redefined and carefully nurtured in a safe and meaningful environment so that we might appreciate an intellect—the teacher's, as well as the student's—in the act of *knowing*. We have to learn to describe the student and the teacher learning. Our task as teachers and writers is to be the narrators of different learning experiences.

Teachers, therefore, must be made accountable for the curricula they develop; they must take care that the environment they are creating for learning is one in which students will have ample time to develop methods of inquiry using various forms of writing—freewriting, journals, creative writing, essays—and various forms of "authoring," including hypertext authoring. Such methods will be characterized by deep reflection, and will allow ample time for presenting the evolution of work, the processes by which the work has come *to be*. This could be done in writing, orally, with multimedia, or by deploying any combination.

To do this we must understand how a single lesson is actually a move toward wisdom. Wisdom, here, is not merely conveyance of knowledge, but rather, an inquiry into our culture's most crucial questions, into our humanitarian pursuit of truth. By describing a curriculum rich in humanitarian concerns, and by describing an environment wealthy in the time given students for reflection and articulation of methods or processes, we will be constructing an environment for inquiry and self-actualization, and therefore for meaningful education.

After students have read, whether Plato or Shakespeare or Toni Morrison or Abraham Rodriquez Jr., I like to ask them, knowing what you know now, how are you going to live the rest of your lives ? We can assess their answer if we know how the teacher's choices of content and methods apply as resources for the student's adventure with this particular question. Again, my argument is that teachers have to narrate their stories, telling readers *why* and *how* a particular classroom looks and works the way it does; we have to be able to fully describe our own learning processes—and how these processes end up informing our work.

In this spirit, then, my choice for using Rodriguez and his short story collection, *The Boy Without a Flag*, was motivated by a notion—an intuition—I had that the students I was teaching, all marginalized for one reason or another, would be able to critique the balance of power in our society regardless of their background, simply because they would see some aspect of themselves in Rodriguez's graphic depictions of poor Bronx life: the entire *system* is laid bare, bottom up: the hierarchy in reverse, the lower rungs perversely working out models created by the upper half.

Further, I believed that students would be able to move beyond a description of the status quo to honest, true wisdom and the projection of themselves into a future they would argue is changeable because of what they've experienced, because of what they've learned, because of what they need—and because of what they've created in this classroom. The expression of their aspirations would simultaneously be a telling reading of the context of their worlds.

This manner of working with students, I thought, would compel them to be accountable to themselves, their ideas, and their beliefs. Students would assume responsibility for their learning because they care deeply about what they say and how they're perceived: they become the subjects of their own inquiries. Thus accountability, we can see in Anton's writing, is self-motivated, taking on the character of true reflection. Anton synthesizes his reading of the world as he experiences Rodriguez's descriptions of the same; he sees and reacts to what he knows, hypothesizing what might be. This is as Socrates suggests: learning is remembering, so our task as teachers is to pose questions that will enable students to recall what they already know. We can describe this; we can determine degrees of recollection, too. A learning curve manifests itself as the student articulates, "this is what I know; and this is how I think what I know will affect what's *to be.*" Anton is seeking to effect change; he wants to put knowledge to work, which is what we want him to experience in education. Anton is taking his world and synthesizing it with the world of the text, creating a realistic vision of where he might be heading. He is slowly redefining our world, discriminatingly.

The teacher intrudes right at the student's injunction, "how I think what I know will affect what's *to be,*" the student's writing itself, challenging, coercing, encouraging—and exposing the larger, historical and environmental contexts encompassing this learning experience. These additions push students to question and perhaps alter their visions, to analyze and to enter into further inquiry about who they are and what kind of world they want to see.

This work also opens up assessment—that too-often dreaded sign of conformity and standardization—to be artfully constructed around and by the student's "organic" *realizations* of his or her reading and writing experiences. Viewed this way, assessment is a natural experience because it is in the student's hands, for the most part. However, critically speaking, it's the teacher who creates the environment that enables this type of "measurement," this kind of "case study" approach to understanding learning that can be later fully described or narrated, as

I'm doing here. It is a quantifiable and creative way to determine what students know, what they see, and then, of course, how they use what they are learning. It's also an interesting way to experience the working classroom. It's more realistic, too, since students are able to move about the information, their thoughts and ideas, and their findings in a multisequential manner, exploring many dimensions simultaneously, and thus really learning: the holds on chronology are therefore broken.

For instance, and in Anton's case, students in a remedial writing course comprised of marginalized students of color and some immigrants, all of whom had been systematically rejected by mainstream society and labeled "minorities" in one form or another, were able to excel in ways they did not expect in spite of an environment that could be initially described, by both students and myself, as extremely negative. Students voiced their "hatred" of their conditions, their hatred of the course, and their hatred of having been mandated into remediation, which reflected their place in society, in the hierarchy. Remediation smacks students in the face, characterizes them as less than, inferior, or problems in the system and society as a whole. The stigma is overwhelming. Most students respond negatively, aggressively rejecting any and all efforts by teachers. It's a vicious and exhausting cycle for all.

To students, the teacher represents the institution that has placed them in this predicament. This was indeed students' first assessment of me. I chose, therefore, to have students revisit their worlds, first by having them reflect on their complex relationships with institutions through focused prompts—family, friendships, community, power, religion, race, sex, gender—then by questioning, exciting, and challenging their reflections and descriptions with a stimulant, literature, which they had all categorically rejected earlier in their education. "I hate to read," and "I really hate writing" was the norm.

Nevertheless, students had to integrate their descriptions of their worlds, as we see Anton doing. Other students did the same with other Rodriguez stories, but for the purpose of reaching beyond what they actually know so as to make critical, insightful comments about the world in which they want to live. This education is therefore purposeful and pragmatic—usable, perhaps. And I dare say, that this experience could be characterized as "just-in-time learning," as well as "preparation-oriented education," the hallmark of the traditional education. It's a hook, actually, for students who have categorically rejected education for one reason or another but now find that they "needs a diploma to gets a job." An education, I want students to understand, is more than getting a job.

This is indeed *a systems approach, a process-oriented system* that takes into account many conditions for learning—the students, the teachers, their respective learning environments, a given department's mission, the institution's mission—characterized by deep, penetrating reflection and critical assessment—and an astute understanding that disparate learning styles must be allowed to flourish.

This *process-oriented system* is indeed quite different, in some respects, to that described above by Elbow. By *process-oriented* I do not mean imposing "a method," but rather, creating conditions in which each student can find his or her own way or methods by which to negotiate the challenges and constraints I place on them. In other words, I am merely replicating how we live: we think, we contemplate, we pursue—and we're challenged on all fronts—so we adjust, we rethink, we, in fact, revise and, perhaps, actually remake ourselves into someone else, another manifestation of our vision. My challenge, the teacher's challenge, is to create an atmosphere that enables teaching and learning and that creates a safe haven in which students can experiment with their ideas, with their methods—with their identities—without judgment.

It is this atmosphere, this *process-oriented* environment, which helps teacher-scholars to begin to understand learning styles, the appropriateness of texts and pedagogies, the context in which students learn. Knowing this enables all of us to begin to readjust the goals and methods of education to meet the needs of our constituencies.

But many of our staid institutions believe this approach is very, very dangerous, because the power inherent in this expressiveness—and in its by-product, artful (self)assessment of the reading and writing act—is in the impressionable student's hands, not really in the teacher's, and definitely not in the institution's.

Certainly there are dangers—for students, which can mean more work for teachers. Maturity, or lack of it, can definitely affect student performance. The more immature the student, the more difficult the task for the teacher, as these students require much more hand-holding, more cajoling. Students can be affected in other ways as well. Marilynn, who I wrote about in the last chapter, actually confronted a teacher during the semester after my course, suggesting to him that his methods were unsound and that he was imposing too much on students because he was telling them how to do things, when to do things, and why to do things. In fact, this professor *was* heavy-handed and very controlling, explaining and determining every single step for students and not allowing them to freely discover ways through questions, confusions, obstacles. He even wanted certain responses, certain "answers," ones that would affirm his sense of self, his role.

Marilynn became the brunt of the teacher's anger, and ended up back in my office, crying, trying to understand her situation. "He hates me. He can't stand me. He's always picking on me," she said disconsolately. "He'll fail me, I know he will." We ended up developing strategies for her that would enable her to finish the course, but without having to experience her teacher's rather vile and abusive reactions to her (he took to ridiculing her in front of the class).

Marilynn survived, having learned Anton's lesson in a different manner—"Many times, we have to go on compromises. We often have to deny ideals so that we can live in peace with institutions." Unfortunately, Marilynn's writing, her work, the journey she began in my class, was momentarily thwarted; she regressed a bit. But Marilynn is a strong and powerful woman, and she persevered. However, others may not do as well; others may regress to *tell me what to do and I'll follow* methods.

Trust has to be a key factor in the classroom I'm advocating. Trust is an instrument for learning.[1] Teachers have to trust their students; trust that students will assume the responsibilities inherent in their own learning; that they will be energetically and completely involved in the inquiry set forth by you, the teacher, since at stake is the context of their lives—of all our lives. Students, likewise, have to trust teachers, an especially difficult task given that this classroom is characterized by "controlled" improvisation, starts and stops—going a few steps back to move forward. And, of course, institutions have to trust their teachers, as well as their students. This is all very difficult because our educational institutions do not invite trust; because we, the professors and teachers, live in a world that is very territorial, very much a world conditioned to worry about "outside" encroachment on our perceived authority. This does not lend itself to collegiality, though collegiality is a category for tenure review.

Then there is the grading factor.

Currently, we appear to grade according to some "standard," which we all assume we agree on, arbitrary though this may be; however, in the classroom I'm describing, grading is quite difficult since there are so many conditions for learning as well as so many different areas in which growth will be experienced.[2]

There's the factor of outside or community criticism.

This type of classroom is anathema to many contemporary models for learning and therefore is readily challenged and questioned from the outside. It's not like anything we've seen before; it's controlled mayhem, I suppose, and the teacher may be the guide, prodding and cajoling, but certainly not "the sage on stage." Defining this classroom, working in this classroom, and even describing and assessing this classroom, is both difficult and time-consuming when one begins the process, though it's more fluid, dynamic, and less time-consuming as one progresses and becomes more comfortable. Throughout the process, however, teachers never fail to understand the potential afforded to students in such an environment, which is a motivating factor for all concerned.

The teacher probes rather than dictates. Many times, to my students' frustration, I find myself saying, "Well, I don't know, why don't you find out and let me know. How would you go about finding out?" Or, as happened when one student, after reading a bit of Aristotle's *Ethics*, declared to me and the class, "This is really hard. I don't know what I'm reading. I don't think I understand. How am I going to understand this?" and I said, "Well, sometimes I too find it difficult to understand exactly what Aristotle is saying, it's confusing to me too." The class panicked, erupted, protested. "You're suppose to tell us," they argued in unison. But this turned into a wonderful discussion about why and how we learn; why we're in college; what our expectations are about education. This was indeed "reflection-in-action." We turned to Aristotle's description of happiness, the one pursuit common to us all, but instead of simply giving them information, they had to do the work required for achieving knowledge; they had to utilize what they already knew, wisdom. They worked through their frustrations with Aristotle's language once they realized they were working through our cultural bias which suggests that *if it's a classic, then it must be hard.*

And, finally, change can be a factor posing some problems as well.

There is in this classroom the potential for changing the balance of power, rearticulating it along lines that are more meaningful, that include thinking laterally, holistically and multisequentially, creatively and enthusiastically—rather than hierarchically. This classroom better addresses disparate learning styles and experiences and thus facilitates the introduction of different forms of stimuli, whether from a text, from music, or from any of the many multimedia forms available to us today. In other words, this classroom affords the potential for change because it accounts for the students' different life experiences outside the classroom. It thrives on students' unique outlooks on life. The student is central to the learning experience, the focal point. This learning environment highlights students' interrelatedness, which in turn emphasizes their responsibilities to themselves and to those that comprise their environment, their community, and beyond.

Essentially, this classroom is a first step in understanding how globalization will be articulated by our students. This is especially poignant if, as Thomas L. Friedman suggests in "A Manifesto for the Fast World,"

> To the rest of the world, American Gothic is actually two 20-something software engineers who come into your country wearing beads and sandals, with rings in their noses and paint on their toes. They kick down your front door, overturn everything in the house, stick a Big Mac in your mouth, fill your kids with ideas you never had or can't understand, slam a cable box onto your television, lock in the channel to MTV, plug in the Internet connection into your computer and tell you, "Download or die." (1999, 43)

Our students' readings of American Gothic as described by Friedman needs to come into the classroom because it's new, it's different, it's challenging—and it's affecting every aspect of our learning, our growth. Likewise, I would argue, Friedman's description makes the development of a truly humanist education even more significant since the "20-something engineers" can't merely "kick down" doors, "overturn everything in the house" and "lock" anyone into anything, though this is their outlook on life, the outlook suggesting that if it's not "programmable" it's irrelevant, bogus.

We have to be able to hear our students. We have to give voice to their voices—then confirm what we hear.

Anton's voice rings out loud and clear. Anton is on his way to becoming an intellectual, if he isn't one already, because he is able to synthesize the knowledge imparted in the classroom with his own experiences and thus re-create this in a description of his worldview. This classroom is a place where Anton finds a type of redemption, a way to come to terms with his identity and his ideals, with socioeconomic distinctions and privilege his readings of his own environment.

Learning is, in part, the process of imposing one's will onto the world and seeing, experiencing, and critically examining how one actually lives amongst and within a context; it is the confident privileging of one's symbolic reading over another's, while acknowledging the possibilities and importance inherent in the multiplicity of readings our American culture is capable of producing—though arguably we may be reluctant to create.

Anton is a working-class student on his way to becoming intellectually autonomous—perhaps capable of enacting change on the ruling class one day. Anton is already cultured beyond our wildest imaginings. Yet he has been labeled "remedial," suggesting that he's "dumber," that he's unable to deal with high-order thinking and complex texts, that he's unable to describe and critique the context of his experiences and, therefore, unable to lend meaningful insight to our culture for its benefit.

Remediation means that the content of the course will be "dumbed down." This means that we don't expect much from them, as was the case with Yesenia, Anna, and Marilynn, and now Anton. If learning means in part that students have to symbolically speak themselves onto the world so that the knowledge they've attained is exposed and re-articulated according to their understanding and vision, then in remediation students are automatically silenced by the notion that they must tell everyone that they are incapable.

Dumbed-down students become puppets to the whims of the powerful; this is costly, I propose.

On the other hand, a classroom can be a place for seeing—analyzing and criticizing, understanding and synthesizing, creating and re-creating, revising. This may be why we've experienced so much resistance to our collective attempts to alter the nature of the classroom: change the nature of the classroom and run the risk of changing the nature of power as we now know it. Today's classroom may give the impression of being a nurturing, welcoming place of creativity, but in many instances, it's nothing of the sort. This view is supported by statistics suggesting national declines in science, mathematics, and reading comprehension standardized scores.[3] However, this can also mean that students can no longer be measured by such bogus vehicles, nor can they be taught in such staid and oppressive environments, which they see as irrelevant. *Teaching to the test doesn't work.* But we know this. Students' worlds are so different from the ones we have imposed upon them in our schools that they are forcibly altering our perceptions of who we are and, more important, where we're heading.

In many instances, we are rejecting our students rather than creating atmospheres for them to re-create their visions of their own experiences in the world we've imposed on them. A healthy, invigorating, and experimental learning environment makes it possible for teachers to synthesize our academic goals and content with the students' knowledge. Their marginalizing experiences combined with their acquisition of "new" knowledge provokes students into a rearticulation—Gramsci's "organic intellectual".

Adding to this is the fact that we, the teachers and administrators—*we authorities*—are rejecting not only our students, but also, tragically and ironically, the means by which to *re*discover our own inner selves and to achieve higher awareness. We are complicit in our own demise. I may quote Freire, who says that "true generosity consists precisely in fighting to destroy the causes which nourish false charity. False charity constrains the fearful and subdued, the 'rejects of life,' to extend their trembling hands" (1972, 29). In doing so, I will be construed as outdated, even overtly romantic and unrealistic, because this is militant 1968 language more consistent with a revolutionary awareness designating the Age of Aquarius. Thus Freire, like other sociohistorical figures, educators, and philosophers, has been relegated to annual academic conferences and forums that merely mimic his teachings and parody his life to create avenues for personal self-gain in an unforgiving marketplace. This is our current prescription for destruction: we, in fact, labor long hours to teach destruction; we major in it.

In this, our current cynicism, Freire might be read as some sort of New Age pop spiritualist rendering null and void lessons we might extract from a problem-posing curriculum. We, then, are destined to continue to "subdue" those "trembling hands," disregarding any and all potential inherent in the human imagination, unless we open up the classroom, with the student as subject.

We have created systems of negotiations and production that are not natural at all because they set as their primary concern the rejection of human imagination and the stupefaction of will—across class lines. No one is pardoned here. But if we provide an environment where students are involved in "reflection-in-action" and "reflection-on-action," we are ensuring that the context of our students' lives, their experiences, will inform our curricula; in turn, the knowledge we are laboring to get across to them becomes more exciting because it's more relevant; it is "just-in-time learning." The teacher's presented content gives students the opportunity to display the context of their own learning and to experience aspects of what they have already articulated, drawing these out, working with them—and adding yet new knowledge. Students can use this knowledge, tweak it, work with it, investigate with it—experiment and expand or recontextualize it. Further, the synthesis stimulates both parties. Students *re*invent themselves and willfully *re*project themselves onto the future in ways they perhaps never before imagined nor believed possible. This is real education.

> We come to know the meanings in language by having heard them from others. Our own experiences add a nuance or a special turn of meaning to what we have heard, which we, in turn, pass on to others. This means that those who have passed language on to us have gathered it from others before them, each passing on the language with a newer nuance. Language, then, is social; insofar as it is social, it is also ideological, carrying various worldviews; and insofar as it is social and ideological, it is also historical. (Villanueva 1993, 85–86)

What I am suggesting is that we first listen to our students' voices to realize, as Villanueva posits, the "nuance(s)" they've added, which have undoubtedly been influenced by TV, videos, electronic games, movies, music, friends, families, or other institutions. We as teachers can then introduce texts as stimuli that bring students closer to our own nuanced readings, however, we have to allow students to freely reexpress their readings, as well as our own, in new formations. These new formations refabricate the social understandings of language; along the way, ideologies may be challenged, changed, ignored, or laid to rest; ultimately, history, as Villanueva informs us, is being revised.

Yet, alarmingly, this neat definition of language and how we pass language on is in jeopardy—in crisis really.

In *The Gutenberg Elegies* (1994), Sven Birkerts poignantly articulates a warning

that the understandings and assumptions that were formerly opera-
tive in society no longer feel valid. Things have shifted; they keep
shifting. We all feel a desire for connection, for meaning, but we don't
seem to know what to connect with what, and we are utterly at sea
about our place as individuals in the world at large. The maps no
longer describe the terrain we inhabit. There is no clear path to the future. We trust that the species will blunder on, but we don't know
where *to*. We feel imprisoned in a momentum that is not of our own
making. (20)

Birkerts worries that without a connection to language and history,
we are likely to be disconnected from ourselves, from the contexts of
our lives, left wondering whether our lives have any contexts at all!

These are desperate, confusing times, made doubly so by our blind
belief that the affluence we seem to be experiencing, at some class levels anyway, is somehow linked to divine providence—bequeathed to us
for our *goodness*, that uses approximately 60 percent of the world's resources to satiate the devouring and purging of only 6 percent of the
world's population. We wallow in affluence's most detrimental by-
product, complacency, to the point of not understanding how vulnerable we really are—everywhere in our culture. These *are* dangerous
times.

We see and understand Villanueva's assertions, and appreciate
Birkerts's warning. Birkerts's paean needs to be heeded; Villanueva's
historical linkage of language, stemming from Bakhtin, also needs our
attention. Because it is here, in these two assertions, that we can find
the transformative antidote to our apparent cultural dissolution: we
must make creative use of "reflection-in-action" and "reflection-on-
action," elaborating on the need for the teacher to first *re*visit herself,
intimately, historically, then, as Villanueva suggests, actively and mean-
ingfully *re*-create herself, "passing on the language with a newer nuance," and so on.

Insofar as this transaction—the divesting or speaking of the self to
students—when it occurs is political and ideological, it enables the creation of a learning atmosphere in which independence and responsibility, creative autonomy, and a strong sense of moral accountability to
the self become the identifiable signs of learning.

True learning comes from one's courage to speak *the self* to others
symbolically. It is a *will to power*. It is also *Renaissance Thinking*. Creating
an environment in which this will take place is the characteristic of a
calling, not a profession. It's a way of life.

These may be dangerous, desperate times, but these are also times
of great opportunity if we learn to think creatively and collaboratively
with our students and with each other. We can indeed transcend the

quagmire of our times and self-regenerate. We can achieve a cohesiveness with our communities and our environment. But first we must realize a cohesiveness with our influences, then speak these creatively to further stimulate "reflection-in-action" and "reflection-on-action" amongst ourselves and our students. This is the only transformative action we have that will negate education as privilege, culture as privilege.

*   *   *

I got my first teaching job because the English department chair at a small, Catholic liberal arts college in New Jersey *assumed* my Spanish name meant that I would have some ease with English as a Second Language students. The moment I stepped into this college classroom it became overwhelmingly clear that the world of graduate school had little or no direct bearing on the needs of my students. The forty or so Hispanic students in my maiden class required work that had no parallel whatsoever with John Milton's *Paradise Lost*, the subject of the master's thesis I had just completed.

I also came to realize that graduate school work, with its intense focus on critical theory and sometimes foreboding manner of reading and writing, had moved me far afield of my reasons for pursuing the study of literature and writing to begin with. I had forgotten why literature and writing are such a life force for me, why literature and writing have always been places that bring understanding to an otherwise confusing world. So to regain this understanding, and therefore bring literature and writing back into my teaching in ways that would become creative vessels for Yesenia, Anna, and Marilynn, for Anton and others, I revisited my introduction to literature and storytelling and re-experienced my early introductions to narratives and their significance—then, and only then, would I be able, I thought, to properly give this same experience to students.

I embarked on a journey that I would later travel again and again with students and would invite students to travel on their own; a journey into nuances and influences. It is a way to realize where I've been and where I'm headed. It is "reflection-in-action" and "reflection-on-action." It's also a journey that, once rearticulated, will become a part, small as it is, of history.

En Argentina Las Pampas are a wide and fertile sea of earth and grasses and life. It was here I learned that a prudent observer can actually experience the subtle rotation of the universe, so plentiful are the earth and the heavens embracing in an expansive horizon. Standing quietly, a spectator is cradled in the soft arms of the universe. One is assured by this.

Las Pampas are the stuff of poetry and adventure; they are impregnated with Argentina's history, its lore, its culture—the good and the bad—its *gauchos*, its Europeanization, and its destructive militarism. They also contain a part of me that I've been forever trying to recoup from afar in my teaching, in my writing, in my life.

I realize this now, as I recall my youth, when I was just an immature boy exhilarated by the blinding experience of life passing through me, like a gushing stream after strong rain.

I was startled from my daydream by the sudden move of my grandfather's DeSoto toward the side of the road. We had been traveling southeast, from Córdoba through Rosario to Buenos Aires, leaving Rio Cuarto to the southwest and crossing a northern most point of *Las Pampas*, its heartland further south nearer Santa Rosa in the province of La Pampa. My paternal grandfather had been filling my head with stories of his ranching days, his stays in *estancias*; how he'd carefully keep track in his *Apuntes*, his diary, the daily events of the *Estancia La Estrella*, "the Star Ranch," he supervised. He spoke to me about the process of branding cattle:

> *the perforation that is almost indistinguishable corresponds to "the sign" of La Estrella, made by the medicated brand with which we try to tattoo the inside ear of the young bulls of "Pedigree." In the other ear we would tattoo the number of the "Pedigree."*

Una estrella, a star:

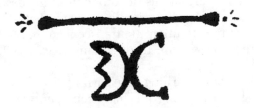

Beginning September 30, 1920, and for an entire year, my grandfather's *Apuntes* are the records of his work as the administrator of the *Estancia La Estrella* that belonged to Dr. Emilio Frers, in San Pedro, a province of Buenos Aires. These *Apuntes* contain meticulous records of rainfall: *Día 10=6 milímetros; Día 26=8.1 milímetros;* temperatures; descriptions of the work: *Día 22—se empeso a cortar alfalfa; se vacuno cerdos,* we began to cut alfalfa; we vaccinated pigs; and the records of deaths: *Día 29, un torito,* a young bull.

The *Apuntes* are a record of my grandfather's life as a rancher, but for me they were the stuff of myth. He filled my head with his descriptions of cattle branding, of hunting *jabalí*, of flying his biplane over *estancias*—skirt down low, just above the grazing cattle, which were indifferent to the intrusion, and heave leaflets announcing fairs or cattle auctions over the side, then sit back on the throttle and reach up, up, and I could see the plane's ascendance with the wave of his hand, hear the sound of the engine blowing from his mouth.

My grandfather's stories, his *Apuntes*, were the beginnings of my literary life because it was at this precise moment I became aware of my imagination, laboring to re-create worlds unknown to me except for the descriptions my grandfather gave them: I was reinventing to suit my needs, from his stimuli. I became increasingly cognizant of the bountiful and unique pleasure associated with creation found really nowhere else.

I was learning quite literally what Emerson says in *Self-Reliance*: "To believe your own thought, to believe that what is true for you in your private heart is true for all men—that is genius . . . A man should learn to detect and watch that gleam of light which flashes across his mind from within, more than the lustre of the firmament of bards and sages" (1960, 147). I came to learn that this Emersonian dictum is at the heart of positive educational experiences. The problem has been how to retransmit, how to transfer this process of "self-reliance" and "self-awareness" to students in a classroom so as to light the fire of creativity and learning.

My love of stories began during siestas with my grandfather, on jaunts into Córdoba from *él barrio* Cofico, during our final trip through *Las Pampas* to Buenos Aires in his DeSoto to meet my destiny in America del Norte. I wanted to tell stories like my grandfather. I studied his manner of holding my attention. He transcended me! In the process I re-created another, new realm through language, as Villanueva suggests it happens.

I was learning about learning, my learning.

My teaching and learning life has been spent reconciling these influences; it has been spent finding ways to work with stories in meaningful ways; it has been spent laboring to understand the permutations of stories, the way narratives recapture and give pause to life's trials, the way a narrative can teach, lend insights, and penetrate mysteries of the heart *because* they are of the heart.

My imagination raced with weather-beaten gauchos, their knives worn to the side and held by a wide sash, coming to a *posada* after a day spent chasing and hunting, *boleadoras* hung over the horse's mane and *panchos* over shoulders. I was startled out of this adventurous dreamland by the car's jerking as my grandfather, *mi papapa*, down-shifted, then eased his DeSoto to the side of the road by a ditch that gave way to a slight stream, barely a scar in the outer reaches of *Las Pampas*.

Without as much as a word he got out and signaled for me to follow. He poised my body toward the steely horizon, leaned over just behind my right ear and raised his arm, asking me by his gesture to follow its line to the tip of his finger.

Beyond what we might normally conceive of as real, as decipherable, a herd of ostrich raced across the long, brown-green grass that was perfectly still in the early morning sun.

It was December, summer, and I had to fight the waves of heat already rising above the grass, releasing beads of glistening dew from their clutches.

Concentrá, he whispered into my ear.

Gradually I began to distinguish their long, still necks; their black, round bodies, feathers coruscating; their barely visible long legs gracefully elevating them above the verdure. They floated effortlessly.

Concentrá. Seguilas hasta que no las ves mas.

Then they were lost, engulfed, like everything else, into the expanse of light, grass, earth and sky.

No, no, no. Todavia no. Mirá. Mirá hacia él horizonte, hacia allá. Tené pasiencia.

Silently I stood fixated on the horizon without as much as blinking. My eyes were dry.

What was he trying to show me? Another animal? Maybe a jaguar? A fox?

I could feel the heat of the sun on the top of my head and the sweat rolling down the sides of my round face. But I did as he said: I stared, I gazed. He kept his left hand on my right shoulder. We were transfixed.

Gently, indistinguishable really, while my attention was on the communion of the earth and sky, I began to notice—I felt—the silence and the motion and the sway, the pantomime of the universe, a soft pitch, a roll almost perfectly still, and familiar.

I stood quietly for some time, mouth agape, sensing nothing but the earth's will.

I looked up and *papapa* smiled down to me and we both knew that the experience had been uniquely ours; that we had been baptized by the universe; that we and the earth and the heavens and each other had suddenly become one. We smiled and without as much as a word slid back into the cracked brown leather seats of the DeSoto, hot on our backs and legs, and gently returned to the ease of the road, *Las Pampas* on either side of us making us aware, poignantly aware of our bond with them, with each other.

This was the first time I *really* thought about dying, that I *really* understood my own mortality, the indifference of the universe. I was certain I had to live fully. I was eleven, almost twelve, on the way back to

America for a second time, this time for good—we were both certain of this. This would be our last time together—ever—we somehow knew this too. It was in the glances we exchanged; it was in this last experience with the earth, *con Argentina.*

Thus myth and lore, language and the imagination, and my own experiences became intertwined, began to shape my world, purposefully and slowly.

I read the entire *Historia de Sarmiento*, the three volumes, and *Martin Fierro*, by José Hernández, the story of Martin Fierro, his two sons, and sergeant Cruz and his son, who suffer the same destiny, the purging of the gaucho's offense that was so attractive to my impressionable mind: a preoccupation with the welfare of comrades, indignation in the face of injustice and the willful and blatant expression of ideas and opinions without fear—the stuff of passionate youth.

I read the Ernesto Sabato of *El Túnel* and *Sobre Heroes y Tumbas*, then Julio Cortazar. Slowly, with age and maturity, the stories of Jorge Luis Borges, the enigmatic literary and cultural influence of so many writers, whether Spanish or not, took hold and left a lasting impression.

> Se debatía el problema del conocimiento. Alguien invocó la tesis platónica de que ya todo lo hemos visto en un orbe anterior, de suerte que conocer es reconocer; mi padre, creo, dijo que Bacon había escrito que si aprender es recordar, ignorar esde hecho haber olvidado.[4]

*   *   *

Literature and life's experiences are interconnected. Out of life emerges literature; literature, in turn, *re*-creates life. Reality, therefore, comes to me in the form of language, symbolically. There are no differences between the language on the page and material reality.

I want students to experience this, to see this—and I want learning to reflect this level of transcendence between the imagination and object reality.

But at age eleven and twelve, I was unknowing, of course, and was led to this awareness by *mi papapa's* romantic approach to life through stories and literature, and by my parent's creation of invigorating learning experiences whereby my expressiveness was occasionally privileged. What I was able to experience was *mi papapa's* own sense that Argentina is a boundless poem, a Borgesian notion I was later to understand. *Papapa* transmitted this to me, to our entire family with his extravagance of character. He lavished us!

In 1963, and two years into my family's original voyage to America for my father's rehabilitation, his attempt to regain what polio had taken away, *mi papapa* published "Como el Hombre del Gólgota! (Leyenda del Altiplano)" in a Córdoba newspaper, *La Voz del Interior*. We had no way of knowing that this story was a precursor to his suicide. We read *Como el Hombre del Gólgota!* as merely *papapa's* flowery parody of his favorite writer, Leo Tolstoy. It is a story of a broken heart; the story of a man who can no longer feel, that *"nada siente, nada le importa ya más."* Nothing mattered to the empty man of the story.

Written in third person it is clearly a narrative mapping *mi papapa's* heavy heart, made so by his having to live apart from his only son, my father, and the family that came to America. We dismissed it as a metaphor for his extravagant nature. But *papapa* was indeed fearful of losing all of us forever.

Now I realize that these feelings of his are what I experienced on that fateful day when he eased his DeSoto off the road in *Las Pampas*: he wanted to leave me with an impression I'd never forget; he wanted to forge a relationship—a unifying bond—between me, him, *y argentina*. He was pleading with me to read it, that's what his face said, that's what his actions said, that's what the land said—though I didn't see it then.

In tragic-romantic form he was trying to teach me a lesson I was not to *re*-learn until Harold Bloom helped me recollect it, enabling connections between my past, present, and future yet to be: "To search for where you already are is the most benighted of quests, and the most faded" (1973, 13). What *papapa* didn't know was that he too was shaping the fabric of my life into stories *through an anxiety* that is *enlightening, instructional, edifying*: "poetic influence scarcely exists, except in furiously active pedants, [and] is itself an illustration of one way in which poetic influence is a variety of melancholy or an anxiety-principle . . ." (7).

It is so that I've come to realize that in *papapa's* poetic refrain, *"No los veré ya más . . . no los veré ya más . . . repite constantemente,"* (*I will not see them again . . . I will not see them again . . .*), exists an illustration of his complete integration of life and literature. Here too he's bestowing me with a poetic influence that is both romantic and perhaps, as it was for Blake, Wordsworth, and Keats, also a tragic sign noting the ending to a particular life-form and the beginning of something else. Life, as the narrator—*papapa*—knew it in *Como el Hombre del Gólgota!* was therefore left for the imagination to *re*-create so as to attempt to *re*live it darkly, ironically, desperately, and figuratively once more before finality.

Life, in some deeply ironic way, is most truly lived through the telling of stories that re-create it.

But *papapa* was unable to tolerate life's trials. *"Vívida y dolorosa evocación . . . ! qué penosa era ahora para él pensar que todo aquello pertenecía al pasado."* How agonizing for him this *vivid and painful evocation*, this synthesis in his memory of grief and foreboding. Everything was now behind him, left merely for recollection. Only death loomed before him.

"*Quiere captar en un instante la visión de sus seres queridos . . .*" To the world he was announcing that his life was now relegated entirely to his imagination, *la visión*, and his efforts were fixated solely on what had been since what was to be, he was certain, was shrouded in a tragic cloud.

In 1968, *papapa* published *La Espera (Leyenda de las "Sierras Grandes")*, a moribund "legend" about a husband and a wife who die and are frozen into a white stone beneath the snow, in the cold, for an eternity, gazing endlessly into the horizon awaiting the return of their long departed and cherished son.

> *Y allí, cerca de "los ranchos de Don Lucas," sobre la chata piedra negra de "El Mirador de los Cóndores" estará por los siglos de los siglos aquella roca blanca, muy blanca, vigilando día y noche, esperando . . . siempre esperando el regreso del hijo idolatrado . . .*

> *And there, near "the ranches of Don Lucas," on top of the flat, black rock of "El Mirador de los Cóndores" will be for centuries upon centuries to come that white rock, very white, watching day and night, waiting . . . always waiting for the return of their idolized son . . .*

Mi papapa signed both stories, *Emil Rehivec.* When he sent us the stories, he sent a key: *Hector Emilio Vîla Regidor*, placing a number 1 beneath *Emil*, a 2 beneath *Re*, a 3 beneath *Vi*, and finally a 4 beneath *Hec*. A code, a sign.

He was trying to tell us something, to transmit something to us in his inimitable way.

In 1973, after we had once again left for the United States, for good this time, and after a short visit to Argentina by my mother, *papapa* writes in a letter to her: "*Cuando me quedaba solo, lloraba tu próxima partida, pero mientras andaba contigo por las calles o negocios, era un custodio de tu persona, de tu espíritu y de tus sentimientos . . .*": When I was left alone, I cried over your next departure, but when I was with you in the streets or shopping, I was custodian to your persona, your spirit and your sentiments . . .

Later he reexpresses his sentiments: "*Nos sentimos muy solos, unidos a ustedes solamente por el débil cordón umbilical de nuestra correspondencia.*" He was feeling alone, tied to his children in America by the "*umbilical cord*" he labels "*correspondence*," a weak link and one that can break at any moment—a sign, perhaps, that the end was near, that he couldn't hold on any longer, that the suffering was unbearable.

Then in the same year, stoically, resoundingly, so it seemed, he writes that "*En mi no se observa el sufrimiento ni los golpes de la vida, pero dentro de mi alma esta todo ello incrustado*": In me one cannot observe suffering nor life's knocks, but within my soul everything is embedded: outwardly stalwart, repressing his emotional downward spiral, inwardly he suffered immensely, irreparably.

In his 1971–72 letters, *mi papapa* was already expressing his regret that he was the subject of my mother's worry, an environment he helped create by his continuous expressions of sorrow due to our departure—a constant source of pain. But now he had a new anguish, my grandmother's cancer, which would eventually kill her, on December 19, 1972—my mother's birthday—after endless operations, hospitalizations, and uncomfortable testing. The tragedy heightened his loneliness, his grief, and his suffering. The pain became unbearable, his solitude confining.

After my grandmother's death and three years of insufferable depression, on April 28, 1975, *mi papapa* went out to the country, to the sierras he loved so dearly and which were a distinct part of his two short stories, and, like the heroine of his favorite novel, *Anna Karenina*, stepped in front of a rushing train.

In the inside cover of a two-volume set of *Anna Karenina* that *papapa* sent my father in June 1974, he wrote that he was sending his son the novel because it brought him back to when my father was but a child, a time when *mi papapa* heaped unbridled love on to his son, a time when *papapa* wrote out his costly, *caras*, illusions. In one of his final letters, a farewell, he writes, "*Un hombre que ha quedado solo, es igual que un desierto*": *A man who has been left alone, is equal to a desert.*

He left behind not a desert but an ocean of wealth. His agony blinded him to the fact that he embodied cultivation. He cultivated his whole family, especially his grandchildren. As Yeats puts it, "A terrible beauty is born": out of life itself has grown an approach to learning, to reading and writing—life-affirming acts. From papapa's death, a life was born.

But many have yet to realize how these life lessons, these affirming acts that serve to teach us and to inform our learning experiences by molding and nurturing our perceptions of the world, can shape our teaching across all disciplines. We have yet to understand, to actually know how to re-inform our experiences into our curricula to foster real-life learning—a living curriculum.

In curriculum development we leave out what we know about the world we inhabit; we stick to formulas and texts and assessment models meant to homogenize our students into forms that conform to the lines along which power is exercised. We departmentalize rather than expand, even though the conditions in our world are asking for *Renaissance thinking*, all-encompassing thinking that integrates our manmade and natural systems: *systems thinking*.

In the chapter "Reading Bakhtin, Thinking Propp" from *City on a Hill*, James Traub erroneously points to a course at New York's City College where a Professor Cappetti is teaching "one of two courses in critical thought required of all English majors" (1994a, 309). Traub quotes Cappetti as suggesting that "in Derrida we have the intention to produce a center without a center, or a structure without a structure—so to speak"; later, Traub also points to the students taking offense when

they read Roland Barthes' "Death of the Author," "as well as . . . an essay by Ian Hunter arguing that not only literature but criticism itself
could only be seen as an unconscious expression of larger historical and
cultural forces" (310).

In Cappetti's class, difficult and challenging material is imposed on
unknowing students and students are asked to react, even to use the
material in any way they can. This method of teaching is attack and
counterattack: the teacher forces arduous, arguably compelling material onto students without framing a context, then the students rebel
or reject the material, closing themselves off, which is followed by the
teacher's, as well as the students', dissolution and the lowering of standards and perhaps the course's scope. Authors such as Derrida, Barthes,
Hunter, and others are simply "given," which means the importance
high culture relishes on these critics is to be assumed, not questioned;
students, most of which come from "challenged" socioeconomic and
educational environments, are expected to understand and use the
materials. The relevance of the material to the students' lives is never
explored. In other words, Derrida, Barthes, Hunter, and others are de-
contextualized. Ironically, Cappetti is working against the themes and
concerns of these philosophers rather than with them, because they are
about inclusion, not exclusion.

Yet it is Cappetti herself who realizes that,

> it's true that these students don't have very much background . . . but
> I think in some ways that they have more of an intuitive understand-
> ing of critical theory because of who they are. These theories deal with
> marginalization and the suppressed viewpoint of the minority, and
> these students are themselves members of minority groups. They
> don't have the sensibility of the dominant group. (311)

My experiences with Anton and those like him compel me to ve-
hemently disagree with Cappetti's last sentence. Our students do have
the sensibilities of the dominant group—they're expressed differently,
that's all. What Cappetti is in fact saying is that she doesn't have a single
notion about how to get at her students' sensibilities. Tragically, Cappetti apparently realizes this and is helpless.

Nevertheless, and even though Cappetti and Traub understand that
there is a relationship between sophisticated critical theory and the
marginalized student, this notion is not used to teach and the class is
rather lackluster, some students feeling that "they had wasted their
time and would forget about the arcane language they'd learned as
soon as the class ended. Others knew that few of their friends would be
willing to endure such an ordeal"; and still others realized that they had
learned how to read differently, how to think differently, more critically, and, in essence, given tools that would enhance their reading and
writing (314–315).

Part of the problem is that we take comments made by students to be rather anecdotal—"they don't know what they're talking about, they're students"—instead of valid expressions of what they're learning—or not. We need to place these reflections within the context of the course for gauging, adjusting, monitoring, redesigning, redirecting, and so on. It's part of *real* assessment.

The students' commentaries in *City on a Hill* suggest that the content of Cappetti's course had very little if any connection with the content of their lives. A fine teacher like Cappetti, and definitely Traub himself, inculcated in classical education models, fail to understand that if there is in Derrida, say, "the intention to produce a center without a center, or a structure without a structure" (310), then something else must assume the locale, the site or foci of the center, even if it's only an impression and ephemeral. It is indeed our intention—both students' and teachers'—to formulate a center, real or not. It's human to do so.

Barthes' "dead author," for instance, is in fact a privileging of reading as a last vestige, or breath, against the inevitable, death. Barthes privileges interpretation because he privileges the contexts of readers' lives, which will certainly affect the context of the interpretation and therefore the text. Barthes is calling for the student to re-create context in conjunction (harmony?) with the text. This is Villanueva's notion of adding nuances to language; likewise, this is a way for Birkerts' lost to find the historical antecedents needed for reprojecting one's self into a future.

Thus, high-octane critical theory or criticism calls for a different method than Cappetti's for the classroom: centralize the marginalized students' experiences as a way to enter complex texts. Since all students, by definition, are marginalized by seeking approval of the educational system, then give them the texts. Students will recognize themselves in what is considered forebidding context.[5]

But first the teacher must speak from a level of experience that will place him or her within (his)her students' circle, thus developing the necessary trust for embarking on such a journey. Speaking with Juliet Floyd, a member of City College's Philosophy Department, Traub finds out

> One day she had realized that most of her class had no idea what a dissertation was, or what it was that scholars did. And so she put off the lesson and talked about graduate school and the life of a professor. "The students were fascinated," she said. Experiences like this made her more certain, not less, that she had made the right choice. (317)

Professor Floyd's right, noble choice may have been to come to City College to serve the underclass and develop a new philosophy department. But she misses the pedagogical approach she's deploying. She is in fact engaged in "reflection-in-action" and "reflection-on-action." No doubt also classically trained, Professor Floyd does not see, or understand apparently, the dialectic she's evoking by easily and honestly retelling herself, recasting herself to her students. She is allowing their imaginations to meet hers, enabling their aptitude to enter her world, her imaginings, the same process she utilized to re-create herself. This is educating with a *real-life curriculum*—but sadly she doesn't see it.

If she would allow her students do the same—take some control over the delivery of material—then Derrida, or Barthes, or Bakhtin, or Propp would be more readily accessible, because they permeate our popular culture in all of its variations. Students would undoubtedly read themselves in the scholarship, as Anton has done. But if she, and others, continue to profess as we did a century ago, we're left with bleak prognostication in the closing of Traub's chapter: "Teachers who knew that they couldn't insist on the highest standards without losing much of their class had succumbed to the ethos of mediocrity that Floyd found so wearisome; they wave as students went on to the next level, still locked in the simplest patterns of thought" (321).

We can do this differently, I propose, and not succumb to such depressing outlooks.

In Anton's Basic (remedial) Writing class, for instance, Panida speaks her mind—in her own voice!—though this voice has been stimulated by Abraham Rodriguez Jr.'s *The Boy Without a Flag*. Panida personalizes her connection to *The Boy Without a Flag*, her sense of how powerful and influential authorities can be, how psychologically intense is the struggle to create an identity for one's self:

> My parents push me to go to school; it is their first priority. They still have hopes of me becoming a doctor, something I gave up on years ago while at New York University when I was a pre-dental major. It was then I realized that I would have to go through a minimum of ten years of school to get to my goal and the thought overwhelmed me.

By making this public declaration to her instructor and fellow students, Panida is able to begin to see, characterize, and enter the role she is rethinking for herself. This learning comes about because, in this class, the instructor created a bridge between the text's context and the students' lives. Professor Cappetti could have done the same; Professor Floyd began, but dropped it. And Traub, reporting and criticizing, gives no hint that he sees anything.

> The teacher needs not only to listen for what has not been said, often out of fear of ridicule, but also to encourage the reflection that produces the most thought-provoking questions. (Grant and Murray 1999, 34)

Borough of Manhattan Community College, a feeder to City College, educates one of the largest minority populations in the country: the student population of the school is 90% minority. And if they're labeled minorities, it also means that they're poor, disenfranchised, marginalized—*of color. The Boy Without a Flag*, in turn, is a selection of very graphic, even sometimes brutal short stories that take place in the South Bronx, an area that has a great deal of crime and poverty. Many of my students were in fact *in* the short stories, which brought to life the students' origins.

Panida writes,

> In *The Boy Without a Flag*, the boy wants to be a writer, but the father discourages it. In school he is taught the lessons of institutionalized power, about order and obedience, and not freedom of thought. The boy ends up confused, not understanding why he would not receive support from both. He tries to fight them and be strong about his beliefs, but he would constantly be discouraged.

In Panida's case, as in Anton's and many others, *The Boy Without a Flag* is a key that opens up their need to express anguish; the text recontextualizes their experiences and enables them to compose their respective theories about the nature of learning, freedom, and their personal existential dilemmas. Likewise, and perhaps more important for the teacher at some level, creating learning experiences that recast the students' lives in different contexts inspires *real-life* learning and encourages them to understand essays and stories from the inside out.

Rodriguez's stories focus on the welfare of children. Readers experience the battle of the sexes and the preconditioning of gender roles ("No More War Games"), the corruptive allure of sexual pleasures ("Babies," "Birthday Boy," "The Lotto"), and the brutality of parents who are hardly older than their own children ("Elba").

After reading these stories, Magdalena, a classmate of Anton and Panida, is prompted to compose a long treatise on abortion, complete with citations:

> In some countries, it is an illegal act; in others, it *is* legal with some or no restrictions; in a few, The People's Republic of China, for example, it *is* mandatory in certain circumstances. Ancient Jewish law strictly prohibited abortion, except in cases where the woman's life was in danger. Abortion was permitted during most of the period that Rome existed. Within the Christian church, abortion has been a sin since the end of the first century A.D.

The brutal depiction of real life in Rodriguez's stories prompts Magdalena to self-question: "reflection-in-action" and "reflection-on-action." The uneasiness she's experiencing, caused by a realism that's not neat and definable and given to arbitrary moral laws, compels her to reach for everything she knows to date so as to *ree*xamine her own persona, the image she believes she inhabits.

Her listing of historical information is Magdalena's method for easing into the subject. Her form suggests an attempt to support her beliefs on the subject; she's conjuring historical antecedents, though she's quite certain that not all conditions will afford her a facile end to her consternation. Magdalena's approach tells us that to be an intellectual and provide a credible argument means to expose contradictions. She's assumed this posture from her *life-learning.* She's speaking this to us in her form.

"Many people," continues Magdalena, "including Stephen Schwarz, the author of *The Moral Question*, believe that the fetus is a person and should be treated with the same consideration as any child or adult."

Magdalena now recalls a conversation with her friend, Maoda, whereby she's informed that her friend had an abortion. Magdalena does not agree with Maoda's choices. "What do you mean you didn't have any choice? You killed your own child," Magdalena rerecords having said in her journal.

Maoda pleads with her, "Do you want me to suffer because I made one mistake?"

Maoda's appeal stayed with Magdalena and was called to the surface when she read Rodriguez's "Babies," so she cites this part of the short story in her essay:

> "Whea's the baby anyway?" I axed, thinkin bout that little dark bundle I saw wrapped tightly in blue at Lincoln Hospital when she had it an I went to visit.
>
> "It's around," she said tiredly, not wantin to talk about it.
>
> "Whea around?"
>
> "I think Madgie's with him outside the bakery. Or maybe I leff him by the liquore store. I dunno." She shrugged like thea was a bug on her shoulder.
>
> "Man, you gotta cut that shit out," I said, without too much conviction. "Yuh a mutha now," I added feelin it was the right thing to say an shit. "You gotta be responsible and take care of your baby."
>
> "I know," she said loud, forehead all pruned up. "I know that! What, chu think I don't know? You think I treat my baby mean? He hangs out with me alla time! Alla time, dammit, he's thea, reminding me!" She lay back on our dinin mat. "Shit. Tell me I don't care about my kid. I bet if you had a kid, you do better?" (46–47)

This final question resonates with Magdalena. Fact is, she's unsure and "Babies" allows her to revisit her position, her treatment of Maoda, her friend. Maoda's world, as it is in "Babies" is perhaps governed by "other," stranger or more difficult, even unforgiving laws Magdalena is trying to understand.

Magdalena adds the following to the above citation:

> Some people believe that both the pro-choice and anti-abortion positions are lacking. For these people, placing abortion in the context of right and wrong lessens the ability for people to make a thoughtful decision about abortion. For them, abortion *is* the taking of human life, but sometimes this decision must be and should be made.

In Magdalena's mind we see unfolding a map of her misgivings. Her writing characterizes Emerson's notion of "Man Thinking," because she is trying to work out her displeasure with the graphic Rodriguez text, her own convictions, history, and her personal life—in a controlled manner. She is learning to use what she is gaining in the classroom; she is experimenting, trying things out. Magdalena is actively engaging her mind with the context of the short story, cited in her essay, and with her sense of history and the literature on abortion—the information controlling the beginning of her essay. But most important, she's engaging her *being* in meaningful ways, as her remarks following her citation of the Rodriguez text show.

Magdalena is speaking what she knows, what she feels, that is, who she is; she's unveiling herself to herself and to us. She is conscious of this. She is achieving consciousness by realizing her identity as it reacts, feels, or thinks when compelled by an object, in this case the text proper. This is not rote learning, but rather, her use of writing to experiment with her convictions and therefore her identity. This is not the use of writing to come to any unequivocal conclusions, but rather, the use of writing to question, to open vistas, to wonder aloud. This is the road to wisdom.

Finally, and as any child of the twentieth century might do, Magdalena succumbs to her sense of the power of science to lend meaning to her inquiries:

> The important thing perhaps, is to emphasize what abortion is not. Abortion is not merely the removal of some tissue from a woman's body. Abortion is not a removal of a living "thing" that would become human if it were allowed to remain inside the woman's body. Abortion is a destruction of the newborn baby! A new human life begins as the egg has been fertilized. Science reveals without question that once the egg is fertilized, every identifying characteristic of a brand-new human being is present, even the color of the eyes. Pregnancy is the period for this new human life to mature, not to "become human"— it already is one. We don't have any rights to deprive him or her of his/her chance to live.

This Magdalena called her "introduction." In essence, as McCormick argues, "it is only when students begin to see that their subjectivities are part of a larger cultural framework that they can develop the skills necessary to evaluate critically the particular positions they take up" (1994, 171). We can see that Magdalena is on her way. In reading Rodriguez, Magdalena entered a contemporary debate, and re-examined a debate within her: she's remaking herself within the context of her learning experience, then expressing her journey in her writing to her audience. In her final remarks, it seems as if Magdalena has made up her mind; however, in her method we see that she's open to considering alternatives, to questioning and to furthering her inquiry.

The important thing here, I'd argue, is that Magdalena has gained an understanding of her method of working through problems presented to her. She's read a provocative text; in turn, she's been asked to reflect on this provocation in her journal, by recounting an encounter or an experience that challenged her point of view: her friend Maoda. Then, Magdalena has been asked to revisit both her experience and the text, the Rodriguez short stories.

Magdalena chose a very logical method; she began with a historical understanding of the subject, moved to the text, citing sections she linked with her journal writing, and then conceded to science in order to justify and support her point of view. She's used everything at her disposal, even beyond what was called for because I never asked for research, and worked her way through the material.

In essence, the problems posed by the assignment's constraints compelled her to reach into her reservoir of knowledge: in her method, her approach, we can come to realize what in fact Magdalena knows, what she's brought to the class. Everything from her past—that she's a woman of color, that's she's poor and disenfranchised, that she comes from a highly questionable academic background, and that she's in remediation—suggests that she should be incapable of doing what she did. But she did it.

Why?

In this remedial, Basic Writing class, Anton, Panida, and Magdalena, among others, demonstrate that they indeed have the courage to speak *the self* to others symbolically. They are therefore learning, *really learning*. They are in charge of their learning. It is a *will to power*: they are learning how complex power's varied configurations can be because I've placed them in the driver's seat: I've created an environment where they can direct themselves—but have to negotiate the constraints placed upon them by the assignment's or lesson's problems.[6] Goethe's dictum begs repeating here: *Art exists in limitations*.

Traub's descriptions and subsequent commentary in *City on a Hill*, however, are about maintaining the means by which power distorts and annihilates the potential inherent in the application of creative limitations, the freedoms. There is something wrong, then, with our collective understanding about how education is delivered, and why it may not work according to our plans. As Theodore R. Sizer notes, we have failed to understand—fully comprehend—what we mean by "school reform" and "school restructuring";

> that there is, in America, an underlying assumption that we all agree on what education is; that there is agreement about standards; and that our leaders believe that these standards must be imposed on an uncaring, unknowing public.

Traub's *City on a Hill* makes these assumptions. I do not. Neither do the students I have had. In fact, what I'm advocating is a reconfiguring of our approaches to literature and writing so that we can begin to understand what our "purposes of education" may be presently.

After all, students, as do I, ardently believe that we are in school for ourselves, for self-betterment, for spiritual and intellectual aggrandizement, as well as for "jobs" and future earnings. We want to find ourselves—then we want to imagine ourselves creatively fulfilled in our future endeavors *in* a community appreciative of our individual talents.

To reach our goals, we can in fact re-create the classroom as a place for seeing and understanding. We can accomplish this across class lines; we can accomplish this in any school, with anyone, if we learn to make the reading and writing acts central to the student's journey into the self within the context of her or his life—and within the context of a dynamic curriculum.

> There are many things that can be taught and learned by practitioners of any craft. Although there will always be an element of the sacred and the intuitive in the practice of teaching, for it shapes the heart as much as it does the mind, the craft of teaching can be analyzed in terms of its essential acts. (Grant and Murray 1999, 31)

Notes

1. For a thorough and creative analysis of "trust" and its relation to "autonomy," no other contemporary text matches *Teaching in America* (1999), by Gerald Grant and Christine E. Murray (Harvard University Press). "Teachers need the proper authority and autonomy to nurture and assess good teaching," the authors argue. "Students will not learn to be creative analysts and problem-solvers if they are taught by teachers who are not trusted to analyze and work out solutions to the problems of their own practice"(3). What I'm arguing for, then, is a process by which teachers will be able to carefully and creatively *narrate* their methodologies so that we will be able to critique, to learn

and understand, to alter and re-define for ourselves; in the process, we will begin to understand the very complex notion of *learning*.

2. Recently, I've been experimenting with "not grading" students, asking them whether they would want me to grade them on every essay they write, or, rather, would they prefer to work with my comments on their papers, assuming from these "how they are doing in the course" and working through on improvements in revisions. If they select the latter method, students are then given the opportunity to write a final, and classic, argumentative essay whereby they describe and self-assess their growth and development throughout the course; I sit down with students and we discuss their essays while examining their portfolios—and I grade them. Or, better said, we grade together, each other (this process, I've found, enables students to speak about how well I've done; what I might do differently next time). I have found that, on average, the student's thinking approximates my own. I have had students come into my office and argue for a "C" because they describe themselves as not having been "all there," not having given the course "its all," thinking that if they would have applied themselves, they "could have done more, been better." So far, I find this method quite refreshing, though, of course, it has challenged an English Department's methods for grading. For a complete study of the theory and practice of responding and assessing student writing, one of the best texts to date, I think, is *Writing and Response* (1989), Chris A. Anson, editor, (National Council of Teachers of English, 1111 Kenyon Road, Urbana, Illinois 61801).

3. According to the *Digest of Education Statistics*, published by the U.S. Department of Education in 1993, the average verbal SAT score for college-bound seniors was 424; Math scores were 478 for the same year. These scores tell two sides of the same story. The first is the apparent lack of a sense of reality—and sensitivity—characterized by standardization's attempt to homogenize learning experiences taking place in disparate environments for students from very disparate—and sometimes adverse—backgrounds: America is not the same everywhere; so learning varies according to socioeconomic and geographic environments. The second part of this story suggests that our students—raised on television, videos, movies, and instructional technologies, in essence, a multimedia definition of reality that is based in economic pressures across all *classes* demanding families separate themselves along profit-production lines—have similar experiences confronting culturally contrived stimuli and thus do not have—cannot have—the learning habits or the interests, *we* may have had at different times. Our students are calling out for education models that are more personable, more closely associated with students' current environmental conditions and conditioning. We are reluctant to provide these environments for a variety of reasons—cost vs. efficiency, the "for profit-only" model, for one; however, we forget that we're in fact responsible for creating the world that our students inhabit, and that inhabits them.

For an interesting treatment of this subject, see Theodore R. Sizer's chapter, "A Story Where Nothing Happens," in *Horace's Hope* (Houghton Mifflin, 1996). "The past decades' hue and cry over the need for high school reform makes sense," argues Sizer. "The existing system doesn't work. What is far less clear—and what there should be substantial argument about—is what should replace the schools we have today . . . What is surprising is that we Americans rarely argue about this—about just what school makes sense—in detail. We avoid the crucial particulars"(16–17).

4. "They debated the problem of knowledge. Someone invoked the platonic thesis that we have already seen everything in a previous existence, luckily that to know is to recognize; my father, I think, said that Bacon had written that if learning is remembering, to ignore is therefore to have forgotten" (*La Noche de Los Dones*, Jorge Luis Borges; translation mine).

5. The notion that we, as teachers, may not be paying attention to what our students are saying or how our students are reacting to our methods is substantiated by Gerald Grant and Christine E. Murray in *Teaching in America* (Harvard University Press, 1999); they are speaking here about Math, suggesting that our practices are pervasive throughout our curriculum: "Depending on grade level, from 61 to 84 percent of U.S. pupils say 'learning mathematics is mostly memorizing.' Although three-fourths of eighth graders report that they participate in discussions about solutions to math problems at least once a week, only a fifth are asked to write a few sentences about how they solved a problem during the week. Even though U.S. students are the most tested children in the world—more than half having a written test every week—they are seldom asked to explain problems to peers or to present exhibits or portfolios (only 20 percent say this happens at least monthly). The traditional written tests usually present the same problems students have solved in class rather than giving students new problems that they must think through using the principles learned" (27). In English composition courses, for instance, this still leads teachers, both in high school and in colleges, to compel students to learn the "five-paragraph essay." My contention is that if we're going to give students "new problems that they must think through using the principles learned," along the way we have to engage in "reflection-in-action" and "reflection-on-action" for the purposes of having students begin an inquiry into their learning methods, describing these for themselves, to peers, and to teachers. Only then will students be able to realize methods that are conducive to a problem-solving curriculum founded on real application of knowledge learned—wisdom.

6. Interestingly enough, in the world of educational technology, this notion of placing students, or participants, into constraints that compel a user to find solutions to problems based on one's knowledge and understanding of his/her environment is being utilized quite successfully with MOOs. For teachers looking for further information on this, some of the best locations are: *http://web.new.ufl.edu/~tari/connections*, for the Connections MOO, and *http://DaMoo.csun.edu:8888*, for DaMoo.

The Student-Centered Teaching Experience

Since I am neither a camera eye nor much given to writing pieces which do not interest me, whatever I do write reflects, sometimes gratuitously, how I feel.

Joan Didion, *Slouching Towards Bethelehem*

The teaching skill lies in the invention of an experience that will do most of the teaching. Extended explanations are unnecessary, although considerable time may be spent afterward in reflecting upon and "unpacking" the experience.

Gerald Grant and Christine E. Murray, *Teaching in America*

We feared Sister Marie Francis in the sixth grade.

At St. Joseph's School, in Garden City, Long Island, Sister Marie Francis, a thin, severe woman with piercing blue eyes made even more penetrating by her black habit, had a reputation for being icy and harsh, a no-nonsense nun who was quick to grab you by the back of the collar, push you up against the wall, and pound your little chest with her long index finger to accent a lesson she'd deliver while bending at her waist and standing so close that she'd spray your face with her spit.

"I—told—you—not—to—talk—in—line," she'd yell, punctuating each word by jabbing her finger into your chest. "What's—it—going—to—take?"

Students stared and giggled and your face grew redder.

I was always in trouble. I don't know if it was ego, aggression, anger, or a combination of all of these, but I didn't fear her. I challenged Sister Marie Francis at every opportunity. I took pride in withstanding her assaults. A quick slap across my face was not uncommon—a daily occurrence. But I persisted.

So Sister Marie Francis took another approach that left an indelible mark on me to this day.

She didn't shy away from the quick slap across the face or the knuckles on the top of my head: these were ways of getting my attention.

"Come up to my desk, Mr. Vila, please," she'd say sternly.

I'd saunter up, still feeling her sting.

At her desk Sister Marie Francis then pointed to a piece of white lined paper. On the top of the paper she had glued a picture cut out of a magazine. These pictures took many forms (I was punished a lot): one time it was a picture of the word *gold*; another time, it was a young girl on a swing dangling from a large tree in a beautiful garden; another picture was of an old schooner.

"I want you to look at this picture and then I want you to write. Build a story that has something to do with the picture."

I understood "build a story." I wrote and I wrote and I wrote. In fact, when the rest of the class was given writing assignments, Sister Marie Francis took to pulling me aside and handing me one of her *pictures on the page* assignments. She'd look down at me with the slightest hint of a grin and what I perceived was a twinkle in her eye that said to me we were involved in something secret, something different and special. I felt important, as if I could do better or I could do things my classmates couldn't. I grew to respect Sister Marie Francis. I learned to behave in her class, though I didn't in anyone else's. Finally, the school's administrators got tired of me and I was thrown out of Catholic school in the seventh grade; however, Sister Marie Francis remains with me to this day. Sister Marie Francis understood a course for my life.

Sister Marie Francis, aside from her proclivity for physical punishment, a hallmark of the Catholic education I was exposed to, created a learning environment for me based on certain assumptions she read from my work, from what I represented. She created assignments that needed little explanation. After school, usually during some sort of detention, we reflected, revisiting my process: I explained what I did, how I did it, and what problems I had had; she, in turn, prodded, gently pushing my attention toward different choices—an odd juxtaposition given her easy manner with physical punishment.

And I wrote again, happily. I revised and worked on other *pictures on the page*.

Now I realize what I felt then: I was at the center of Sister Marie Francis's attention. Sister Marie Francis's *pictures on the page* assignments were characterized by her trust in me. I felt that she believed in me, an especially poignant lesson since my reputation in the school as a notorious troublemaker (I'm being mild here) bordered on the mythic: I was not allowed to go on school trips; I spent lunch periods in Mother Superior's office; I lived in after-school detention. Literally, I was an outcast, a position, I might add, I helped to bring about and, in all honesty, relished. Sister Marie Francis, however, placed me in a creative center; she let me go on my own: she trusted me—and this went quite a long way with me.

I now also realize that my troublemaker demeanor, besides having something to do with my father's polio and all it entailed, had much to do with my need to do things for myself, to find my own way and be on my own, regardless of the obstacles. I have come to believe that this notion of grappling with life's challenges in order to be self-determining is a uniquely human conviction, a kind of inalienable right; more specifically, self-determination and self-reliance are fundamental to the American experience. I bring this into every class I teach.

I wonder, for instance, why Sister Marie Francis didn't provide the learning experiences she gave me to everyone else? Why was she so adamant about physical punishment, though in my case an alternative tack worked better? Did she not see this alternative as appropriate for everyone else? What was it about her influences—religious or otherwise—that compelled Sister Marie Francis to actually separate the class by giving different learning experiences to different students? What, in fact, did she represent? Catholic education? Education as a whole?

I suspect that Sister Marie Francis believed that she was somehow upholding a value system. I, however, don't necessarily perceive myself as being a teacher who steadfastly upholds the values of a culture or an institution, though certainly in my manner and in some of the texts I select I am certainly defined as a stalwart member of an institution. I'm sure I'm perceived this way by many students, especially as I age. So I understand that one of the things I must do in the classroom is challenge a student's outlook concerning the perceived wisdom of his or her society—an "iconoclast," a student once wrote of me in her review of a literature course I taught.

This line of thinking, I believe, is extremely important in remedial courses because the pervasive institutional and cultural notion about students inhabiting this no-man's-land is that they're incapable—of anything—and certainly not able to work with college-level materials. These ideas are counter to my way of thinking; they are contradictory to my very core.

My experience tells me that students, regardless of their background and (lack of) preparation, can work with stimulating and dynamic material. However, it is incumbent upon the teacher to create a learning environment that will nurture as well as challenge students, particularly those that already appear in our classrooms with feelings of inferiority, with a reluctance to explore and inquire, or with bogus notions about their capabilities.

Students in remediation have had an educational experience that has inculcated in them the idea that their role in the classroom, in the institution itself, is merely to regurgitate the information given to them by teachers. They have been trained to follow. Essentially, students in remediation have been schooled: they've not been exposed to education, nor have they been educated; they've been involved in schooling, which is political and subject to gross manipulations. This means that they are averse to learn on their own; hesitant to question and experiment. They don't know how to take control of their learning. They therefore expect the teacher to tell them what to do and how to do it, how to take and pass the dreaded WAT, for instance. They want to be told how to advance. Education, for them, is seen as a series of obstacles that must be overcome for advancement, a hierarchical world that finds students, perhaps even teachers too, on the bottom rung.

For a teacher, this is a difficult position: on the one hand, the system dictates that students will not move forward unless they pass a standardized test that actually measures absolutely nothing; on the other, the teacher knows that writing is much more than merely passing tests—it's a way of thinking, vital to inquiry and exercising the imagination in uncharted realms, and it's a way to maintain the vitality of learning throughout one's life.

Teachers want success for students well beyond the classroom. So, faced with a test that arguably says nothing about a student's ability to think and write—and is an obstacle to critical thinking and creative, intelligent writing—I decided to cheat.

It's easy to cheat the system by teaching to the test; teaching to the test, or mind numbing, is the easiest exercise a teacher can perform. I therefore developed a process: I was certain that if I gave students very difficult but stimulating work throughout the semester, their writing would improve in meaningful ways; they would notice things, understand things about their writing that would make the taking of the WAT easier. Students would be able to contextualize the idiocy of the punitive exam, demonstrating an understanding of the difference between writing-to-learn and writing as a means of responding to an institutional mandate or to give approbation to rules of discipline. Because the WAT is meant to endorse administrators who like to equate the standardization of the educational experience with real learning.

I knew I needed approximately ten to fifteen days to teach to the test, since I was only giving them a formula, a schematic of test taking after the grueling and challenging semester's work. I was cheating the system, perhaps, but in the process my students were being exposed to two worlds: the world of learning, of inquiry, of achieving an identity by writing; and the vituperative, political side of educational institutions, schooling.

*   *   *

I gave my remedial writing class a word, *romanticism*, then let them explore and experience by writing—and eventually they created a picture.

Willie, an Hispanic Asian American from Brooklyn who always came to class dressed in battle fatigues and combat boots, a metaphor for how he views his journey through life, wrote: "A feeling. For someone else. You want to give everything to the person. Its natural."

I then asked about the difference between "being romantic" and "romanticism": what does it mean to add an "ism"?

"Romantic is when your really into it," Willie wrote in his journal.[1] "The other one is when society agrees."

Actually, no one in the class had any problems differentiating between the active, "being romantic," and the static, institutionalization of the active into an "ism." These students experience "isms" as somehow relegated to "society," their favorite, universal word when no other became available for defining an abstract idea. An "ism," they expressed in unison, encompasses all of us.

Following the "romanticism" prompt and a brief discussion about what the students had written, I gave the class a packet labeled English Romanticism Project. (My sense, here, is to give prompts—stimuli—to get the mind set and establish an atmosphere, then to give materials to further push what the students are already saying or admitting to. I give little or no directions, but continuously ask students to write and rewrite, compelling them to revisit what they've already written, to question, and to revise. I expose or peel layers so that students have no other choice but to think, inquire, and write to find their way. I am keenly aware that as a teacher I'm more like a narrator: I describe scenarios, conditions, and tensions, give problems and conflicts, and draw lines, but I don't connect them; rather, I let "reader-students" make connections for themselves and, most important, note where they see the connections.)

The English Romanticism Project packet includes poems by William Blake ("The Lamb," "The Tyger"), William Wordsworth ("My Heart Leaps Up When I Behold," "The World is Too Much With Us"), Lord Byron ("She Walks in Beauty"), Samuel Taylor Coleridge ("Pantisocracy"), and John Keats ("Ode to a Nightingale"). And I outline a series of tasks: Go to the library and find a book, an encyclopedia, or another general reference text and look up English Romanticism; Select one major contributor, whether literary, political, or religious, and give a brief biography so we can better understand what was being said about the period; Read the enclosed poetry and write, in detail, your reactions; Go to the library again and find some details about one of the poets read; In anything read, do you notice any parallels with your own life?

The packet also begins with a statement I've written:

> The bulk of literary work known as English Romanticism falls between 1789 and 1832. Romanticism began and prevailed in a spirit of revolt against the dogma of reason, or against the actual or supposed neoclassicist conception of it.

After students write and speak about "romantic" and "romanticism," I want them to sit with this type of stylized rhetoric before seeking sources. I see it as a juxtaposition to their own definitions: *what you said isn't wrong, but here's another way to put it*, I'm suggesting with my statement. I want them to experience the language of the academic, the language that can be a mote meant to keep away, rather than include, certain types of people—or as Yeats says about uses of Plato, Aristotle, and Pythagoras by teachers in "Among School Children," *Old clothes upon old sticks to scare a bird*.[2]

In their research, and certainly in their continuing journey through academe, they will confront this language. I want them to feel my trust in their ability, so I hand them their English Romanticism Projects without saying a word. I need to understand—to see—how they will negotiate the language. And I want them to see that I have trust in their ability to do so.

"The list of things to do" is given to keep students on track. Since my purpose is not to teach research, though certainly some fundamental principles apply, I want to give them the confidence to work with college-level materials on their own; to give them the same opportunities nonremedial English students have, to level the playing field a bit, to envelop them in an inquiry of a specific and most likely alien subject as well as themselves. I want them to say, "Aha, yes, I see myself in this material. It's not foreign to me at all." I want them to begin to learn to find themselves within this alien, academic world of rules and ominous language. Ultimately, I want these students to experience the relationship between academic rigor and accomplishment by doing.

Predictably, students looked at one another. *This must be another one of Vila's crazy assignments*, their looks said. This class had experienced my Inner/Outer work a couple of times; they also had completed "The Crito" work described earlier, so there was already a foundation for working with primary texts.

The English Romanticism Project was their fourth assignment, a continuation of the process of moving students to become independent thinkers, of challenging their notions of "schooling," and of reconceiving themselves through education—most important, writing.

Young students in elementary school are inevitably exposed to poetry, even asked to write poetry, which they relish; however, some time after this early experience we categorically disassociate poetry from their learning, and it becomes bile. Then, once students become juniors and seniors, they are typically asked to read "Romeo and Juliet" and "Julius Caesar." Small wonder they see Shakespeare as punishment, as another obstacle in the advancement game.

Students have plenty of poetry in their lives. They experience their lives poetically, for the most part, so it's simply a matter of presenting a learning environment where their poetic memories can be reawakened. Similarly, I believe that all students would appreciate romanticism, since human passions, revolution in the face of injustice, and our need to feel a deep, abiding relationship with Nature are universal, and perhaps particularly poignant to remedial students from marginalized existences.

Willie, for instance, followed a trail that began with an encyclopedia and ended up with the *Introductory Survey of English Romantic Poetry and Prose* (1979), by Russel Noyes. He read it. It is instructive to examine Willie's journal notes on his way to his essay on romanticism and William Wordsworth.

Willie's eye initially caught the relationship between romanticism, revolution, Europe, and America—and his education:

> I don't know if I forgot or I never learned it. "Political revolution dramatically broke loose in America with 'the shot heard round the world' at Lexington (1775) and in France with the Storming of the Bastille (1789)." So it means folks were pisst off for a long time ago. Nothings new.

From revolution, Willie turns to Nature, realizing that,

> Maybe we live to complicated. In NY its yes. It says that "The return to nature for the romantic generation not only meant a new delight in external nature but also involved the belief that natural, or earliest, conditions of man and human society are the best conditions." We said in class that this was what part of the 60s might be about. My father went to Nam. I feel like I'm suffocating sometimes.

He then goes on to cite from the *Introductory Survey* that, "The first romantic element which comes into prominence is a new awareness of external nature," as if to accent his earlier statements. This quotation Willie lets stand by itself. It's underlined too.

It's interesting to see what Willie is noticing, especially after his initial understanding that "being romantic" somehow involves "a feeling" and that this feeling "is natural." Willie is searching for connections, first by noting that revolution, romanticism, and America are closely related, therefore there must be some relation to him: "Nothings new" could be seen as an assertion about his understanding of history as an ongoing condition.

Willie then perceives a relation between this *naturalness* and his sometimes feeling as if he's "suffocating," a notion brought about by his reading of the "natural . . . conditions of man and human society" as being "the best conditions." He reads his condition as not the best, nor ideal.

Willie, I'd argue, complete with his urban warfare outfit, has entered the romantic persona, the romantic paradigm, a sense that there's something "off" with his current experience and that there's perhaps some ideal or something more meaningful to experience.

We can even extend the analysis to suggest that Willie is a bit uneasy. Willie continues to cite: "a preference for urban to a love of country life, natural scenery, and solitude." Then he writes, "I like being alone. I'm alone all the time."

Finally, when Willie gets to the section titled *Romanticism* and completes the *Introductory Survey* of *English Romantic Poetry and Prose*, he notes that,

> When I first wrote about "romantic" I thought it had something to do with how you feel about someone. Like you love someone. How I feel about my girlfriend. Now I'm not so sure. It says that "It originally meant 'like the old romances,' but since these works had to do with improbable adventures remote from ordinary life, 'romantic' came to mean something unreal or far-fetched." Vila asked us if romantic was some ideal. I think that when you first fall in love with a girl you tend not to see. Love is blind they say. Then she gets old and fights start. It's over.

It's not surprising, given Willie's propensity for the personal as it comes into conflict with ideals that he would select William Wordsworth for his formal writing. Willie's first journal entry on William Wordsworth is a citation he places on the top of the page, like a title:

> He brought renewed worthiness to English poetry by dealing directly with human passions, human characters, and human incidents.

Our class discussions evolved around what students gathered in their research, their citations, and their reflections. Students moved the class along. Each class period, we discussed, wrote, and worked in groups on grammar and editing, though some of this work was done with me solely. Sometimes, grammar requires a class discussion on a fine point.

My role, whether as a writing teacher or as a literature teacher, is to add the missing pieces *after* students expose what they understand.

Then we read the poetry.

My tactic is to read a poem through entirely, stop, then reread the poem, slowly, and ask questions in a manner that excites discussion. Naturally, having attained some background understanding from their research, students are able to see the major themes in the poetry. They make connections easily. The more subtle nuances of the poetry need to be teased out in-depth during discussions. I also have students volunteer to read some of the poems. Only a few participate, which is, I think, understandable. My motivation for the class discussions of the poetry is always to add depth to the writing.

The following is Willie's introduction to Wordsworth's "My Heart Leaps Up When I Behold":

> When you think of Wordsworth's belief in nature and man's soul you can see how he could write a poem such as "My Heart Leaps Up When I Behold." A rainbow in the sky, young and old, father and child describe a theme about nature. Wordsworth explains how his love for nature goes to the extent of feeling refreshed whenever he sees the beauty of nature. If nature were to be stricken from his eyes then he'd rather die. "Or let me die!" he says. (1.6)

In one of his journal reflections about the romanticism assignment, Willie stated that this work felt "like real college." I believe we can see evidence of this in Willie's essay, an attempt to lodge his world into his learning:

> As every new period or era is a revolution, so is Romanticism in many ways. With new ideas of expression and new techniques comes disapproval. This marks a revolution. This revolution for free expression parallels many feelings of artists today. Although I haven't seen it with readings except for comics or porno magazines, it is most obvious to me with music. Rap and heavy metal are individualistic expressions. Just as jazz or salsa would be to others. With so many types of music performed by so many different people, who can say this is not individual expression? Why else might two people like the same type of music but not the same group?

Although awkward, stiff even, Willie is trying to make his voice formal: the voice of the academically accepted, the assimilated. "Rap and heavy metal are individualistic expressions." He's struggling to take on the persona of "the student," as Yesenia did. He is wrestling with large and important issues, too: "individualistic expressions," "revolutions," and the private versus the public, the notion of societal "disapproval" of one's expressiveness, a common occurrence for the disenfranchised in Brooklyn. "With so many types of music performed by so many different people, who can say this is not individual expression?"

In Willie's lines is also the dilemma of self-esteem and self-regard Cornel West speaks about in *Prophetic Thought in Postmodern Times* (1993). Having never felt accepted by the mainstream, Willie is hesitant in this new form; he's never experienced himself trying on the language of the "establishment," the "cash language." Since it's a matter of acceptance for Willie, he has to first overcome feelings of inadequacy that have been inculcated in him from birth in order to achieve fluidity and comfort in the form. The syntax is rigid, as if he's trying to hold back, or keep something away—or maybe he's adjusting to the fit, trying to understand where his identity might be in this foreign world. He's learning to put on these new clothes, while simultaneously attempting to assert himself and not lose what he already brings into this once forebidding rhetorical form.

Willie's progress toward the creation of his essay was painstakingly slow and arduous, not because he "couldn't do it," but because of how he felt about himself as a learner. Tragically, he was scared to actualize himself in his learning. He was trying to keep at bay ill feelings he undoubtedly experienced before in the act of learning. The entire class, me included, had to do a lot of urging, a lot of "come on, Willie, it's okay, try." We all, in fact, needed each other for this journey.

Where did Willie's spirit for experimentation get squelched? Does all of society have a hand in nurturing this fear?

Willie writes:

> William Wordworth's feelings of a tie between nature and man's soul are strongly agreeable in my own mind. Because as time goes on and man continues to rape the earth it is dying and so will we. Only when nature is respected by man will we be able to flourish from its nourishment. We have to first respect each other.

It's difficult for Willie to work syntactically with these intense ideas; he's never been called to do so, he told me. Yet we still get a sense of how bleak, though perhaps prophetic, his ideas are. Willie is now ready for a deeper immersion. Hawthorne maybe? Wallace Stevens? But will he be exposed to more of this type of work as he moves from remediation to yet another "standard"? If he has not been asked to do this kind of work before, and Willie is twenty-two, will he again?

If we consider what Cornel West says, that "You can still get tenure in some universities for arguing that black people are not as intelligent as others" (1993, 11), then Willie probably won't get Hawthorne, or Stevens, or anyone else for that matter. Giving him hope and a future is not politically expedient. In some neighborhoods it's honorable to go to prison; it's a badge of courage. It's even honorable and heroic to die.

So what are we saying?

Cornel West puts it best:

[T]he major challenge presented to black America, to black scholars, black intellectuals, and to black leaders and black people. And the challenge is this: 1) it has produced the highest level of forms of self-destruction known in black history. And these demons which are at work, the demons of meaninglessness, of hopelessness, a sense of nothingness conjoined with the institutional and structural marginalization of large numbers of black people, though not all . . . But, for the most part, it has produced the highest level of self-destruction known to black people since we arrived. And the reason why is because for the first time there are now no longer viable institutions and structures in black America that can effectively transmit values like hope, virtue, sacrifice, risk, of putting the needs of others higher or alongside those of oneself. (150–151)

I'd add that in all America, black and white and in-between, there really are no institutions that "effectively transmit values . . ." This is Willie's world, our students' world, our world.

"The main thing I feel that could be done to further my status in writing is to explore more topics because the more interest you have in someone else's writing," says Willie in his portfolio's self-assessment letter, "the more you might gain in your own." He's not sure if he will get more of "someone else's writing"; his "might" gives rise to the uncertainty. Willie knows one thing: how the system works: it's not systematic and the chances that he will continue to get work similar to that which he received in this remedial writing course are slim to none.

So I push. And move away from literature, shifting the ground beneath what I perceive to be the students' growing complacency in the course—their collective sense that we'll be writing, reflecting, then reading Literature to then create essays—and turn to statistics and our cultural attitudes and behaviors as expressed in charts, tables, and numbers—a different type of storytelling.

On the heels of the romanticism work, I ask students to spend some time with the following terms: *family*, *community*, *marriage*, and *children*. In this sense, and after an inquiry into the romantic spirit, dealing with ideas that are closer to home, such as *community*, *family* and *children*, I'm asking students to delve deeper, to move further into themselves, to find yet closer, more direct connections with the larger, complex world.

By now, students write and share and speak simultaneously. They're a noisy bunch. It's the noise of comfort, ease, and confidence. As we discuss these terms, I do "active listening" and record what students are saying on the board. I don't criticize, nor do I judge. I urge. And dynamically repeat what students say as I compose for all to see.

"So you're saying that a family can be comprised of friends, people in the building you live in, perhaps people not even on the same floor?"

We have a community's sense of our thoughts, of learning.

Comparing the State of Children

A study of American children shows that their
environments have changed in several important areas

1960		1990
5%	Children born to unmarried mothers	28%
7%	Children under 3 living with one parent	27%
90%	Children under 3 living with both parents	71%
2%	Children under 3 living with a divorced parent	4%
Less than 1%	Children under 18 experiencing the divorce of their parents	Almost 50%
17%	Mothers returning to work within one year of a child's birth	53%
10%	Children under 18 living in a one-parent family (approx.)	25%
28/1,000	Infant mortality (deaths before first birthday)	9/1,000
27%	Children under 18 living below the poverty line	21%
18.6%	Married women with children under 6 years old in labor force	60%

Without as much as a word, I hand out a statistics sheet, "Comparing the State of Children," published by the Carnegie Corporation Report and referring to work done by the U.S. Census Bureau, the Urban Institute, and the National Center for Children in Poverty.

With the "Comparing the State of Children" material, as well as the work with the Abraham Rodriguez Jr., short story collection, *The Boy Without a Flag*, I've been accused by some colleagues of pouring salt on open wounds. "Why would you give these kids such inflammatory materials?" colleagues have said. "I could never ask students to work on materials that might excite them, rile them up. They live in these worlds. Why would you point this out to them?"

It is precisely for these reasons that I have worked with provocative material. We've skirted the issues and conflicts of marginalized students of color in the classroom for far too long. And I'm not from their world. I need to learn about my students so I can better address their needs. Students also need to see that their lives are being talked about, measured, and analyzed in public forums. I want them to speak up about their long-muted experiences; their voices need to be let into these conversations. I am opening up conflict(s) as a way to learn—and gain power.

In her portfolio letter, Maricela, an Hispanic student, writes:

> As I went along in my writing course at Borough of Manhattan Community College, I managed to get a much better understanding of how to improve my grammar and future compositions. I have to admit, I found the course to be very difficult at first. I even began to doubt my ability to proceed in the course, but I did. Sharing my work with my fellow classmates, I noticed everyone felt the same way I did, which gave back my confidence. The class worked together and we made each other more creative in our writing.

Battling private feelings of inadequacy stemming from her history and the predominant obstacle to learning in remedial writing courses, Maricela is able to grow and find "my confidence" in the communal aspect of the classroom, realizing that working together "made each other more creative."

The ways in which the dominant class proceeds and succeeds—team work, interesting and invigorating challenges that excite the imagination, clean, safe learning environments with plenty of time for experimentation, trial and error—are never shared with those less fortunate like Yesenia, Willie, and Maricela, and the other BMCC students.

For instance, Maricela notes the importance of revision in her process almost as an epiphany:

> My writing has improved in many ways. One way is being on track and sticking to my ideas and point of view. I kept writing, erasing and rewriting, writing and rewriting, like a cycle. By doing this, I learned to go over my writing and have the ability to find and correct my grammar.

Maricela announces that she would "like to improve my writing even more to the extent that I can be able to be an excellent creative writer. In my work I want to be able to express my points clearly and concisely."

In "Then and Now," Maricela's essay on "Comparing the State of Children," she works very hard to be clear and concise. We can see her struggle with syntax, as she attempts to be authoritative while drawing from her personal experience raising a child as a single mother.

> It is very important for children to have both parents living together because they need the love and the affection of both. Children always need attention and it's always healthy for the child to have these important qualities from their parents as they are growing up.

"Comparing the State of the Children" was one of the final two formal essays in the course. I knew that the greatest difficulty for students would be in translating their statistical observations into meaningful points of view. But I also felt as if I'd already worked through various techniques—brainstorming, prompting, group work on outlining, and editing—that would enable them to find their own way.

Maricela, for instance, noted in her journal and in comments to the class the difference between her upbringing in Puerto Rico, on a farm with both parents, and her own situation as a single mother raising her child with the help of both of her parents now that they, too, had come to the United States—"the mainland" she called it. Thus when Maricela reads the statistics, she makes assumptions about what she perceives as another generation's morals:

> Times have changed from 1960 to 1990. The family was very important in the 60s. It was also important keeping it together. Children did not experience the divorce of their parents as much as they are experiencing it today. In the 60s families were kept united; not putting kids through rough stages was very important then.
>
> Statistics show that in 1960, 17% of mothers returned to work within one year of a child's birth. It increased in 1990 to 53%. When a single mother is put to take responsibilities over the household expenses, it is very difficult to get financial support. The fact that more children are being born to unwed mothers, puts mothers in a position in which they are forced to work to support their major needs. The child begins to grow up feeling depressed and lonely, even seeking the affection of a stranger.

Late in the term Maricela is still struggling with many aspects of her writing: she's trying to synthesize her beliefs with her situation (which, we see, challenges her morals); she is also trying to fit these conflicts into a coherent essay. And she is working her reading of the "Comparing the State of Children" statistics into her writing. The result is the somewhat stilted effect of statements she feels she must make in order to appear the voice of authority. "The family was very important in the 60s. It was also important keeping it together."

But we can also note that Maricela has an intuitively subtle rhetorical strategy. This is her strength, a starting point for growth and development; this is her foundation. She quickly establishes the importance of family life, especially as it affects children. She declares her position: "It is very important for children to have both parents living together because they need the love and the affection of both." Maricela has experienced this, so she realizes that somehow this may be lacking in her daughter's life: "The child begins to grow up feeling depressed and lonely, even seeking the affection of a stranger."

She even digs herself into a hole, or perhaps she's examining her position honestly, going deeply into a position that contradicts her own existence: "Children always need attention and it's always healthy for the child to have these important qualities from their parents as they are growing up." Though her language is not quite there, we understand what she's trying to say. Maricela is agonizing over complicated ideas that challenge her limited vocabulary. English is Maricela's second language and we can see how difficult it is for her both to deal with the language and simultaneously to attain the pitch of the academic essay.

Clarity, Maricela senses, begins by trying to glean insights from the statistics: "Children did not experience the divorce of their parents as much as they are experiencing it today." For Maricela, it is point, counterpoint; contradictions, juxtapositions. "When a single mother is put to take responsibilities over the household expenses, it is very difficult to get financial support. The fact that more children are being born to unwed mothers, puts mothers in a position in which they are forced to work to support their major needs." Women like Maricela are heads of households; likewise, they are mothers—and the two, in her mind anyway, are somewhat paradoxical. The outcome is that, "The child begins to grow up feeling depressed and lonely, even seeking the affection of a stranger," so the meaning of "family" is extended or altered.

My goal is to expose Maricela and her classmates to a variety of difficult, college-level work in order to solicit the fundamental ability they possess to assume a persona through language in order to assimilate into the dominant culture, the culture that dictates and sets the conditions; the ability to begin to at least mimic this language, and thus gain a clearer picture of a learning trajectory they need to follow. These students need to know where they are and they need to know where they have to go; the journey must be made visible and attainable.

For college students, it's not enough to merely learn English. They also have to begin to understand the language of academe in order to enter into disciplines that will best accommodate their need to work creatively in language-forms such as mathematics, engineering, medicine, education, law, architecture and arts. This will give them a more even chance to best articulate their identities and achieve their dreams.

Gaining the needed confidence to surge ahead in years yet to come in higher education is achieved by respecting remedial students—and this requires exposing them to stimulating and sometimes difficult material. We must trust they will recall the strategies they learn when confronted by difficult learning situations.

*   *   *

The final project of the course involves Shelby Steele's essay, "On Being Black and Middle Class," a provocative criticism of the black experience in America as examined through our notions of *class*, the unspoken subject in our society.

During this work, I'm very much on the periphery, enabling students to control the discussion and the writing, commenting on what they select to be important, and even allowing them to choose their own working partners for editing and revising. Students take turns writing on the board during "active listening" as well: in all, I am deliberately ensuring that students take total control of the class, reaching into their knowledge base to complete their essays.

I want students to experience ownership of their learning— completely.

Fading is the healthiest act a teacher can perform in a classroom. This is the goal of teaching: to reach a point where the teacher is not needed and therefore becomes a co-learner, another student; where students find the will, as well as the means, to be self-motivated learners—and therefore teachers themselves.

I was taught a lot by my students and, as is evidenced in this *narrative*, I have learned plenty, but especially in this final exercise. The first thing I came to understand, immediately, was how much the students agreed with Steele. They too wondered why they had to celebrate the black underclass as the "purest" representation of African American experience. Students wanted to steer far afield from the "victim-focused black identity" Steele describes:

> Not long ago, a friend of mine, black like myself, said to me that the term "black and middle class" was actually a contradiction in terms. Race, he insisted, blurred class distinctions among blacks. If you were black, you were black and that was that. When I argued, he let his eyes roll at my naiveté. Then he went on. For us, as black professionals, it was an exercise in self-flattery, a pathetic pretension, to give meaning to such a distinction. Worse, the very idea of class threatened the unity that was vital to the black community as a whole. After all, since when had white America taken note of anything but color when it came to blacks? He then reminded me of an old Malcolm X line that had been popular in the sixties. Question: What is a black man with a Ph.D.? Answer: A nigger. (1995, 27)

Students were excited by Steele's voice. What Steele is saying touched their innermost thoughts about *class*, race, and their identity. Steele opened them up and gave them permission to make meaningful declarations about how they felt concerning their experiences as *minorities*. Steele became the teacher I could not be for this work. Truly, the class belonged to the students. They spoke to each other, and to Steele.

They had never been exposed so openly and publicly to this "dialectic," as Steele calls it.

> Being both black and middle class becomes a double bind when class and race are defined in sharply antagonistic terms, so that one must

be repressed to appease the other . . . Identity is not the same thing as the fact of membership in a collective; it is, rather, a form of self-definition, facilitated by images of what we wish our membership in the collective to mean. In this sense, the images we identify with may reflect the aspirations of the collective more than they reflect reality, and their content can vary with shifts in those aspirations . . . One might say that the positive images of one lined up with the negative images of the other, so that to identify with both required either a contortionist's flexibility or a dangerous splitting of the self. The double bind of the black middle class was in place . . . (29)

Brian was compelled to note the trajectory of the black experience as it had been told to him, or as he understood it. In so doing, Brian was laboring to identify with a resounding theme in Steele's essay he felt describes his own conflict. Steele notes that, "Still, hate or love aside, it is fundamentally true that my middle-class identity involved a dissociation from images of lower-class black life and a corresponding identification with values and patterns of responsibility that are common to the middle-class everywhere" (31). Though Brian and his classmates had not grown up with swing sets in their backyards, as in Steele's case, they identified with the author's sense of self, his embrace of middle-class values and life.

The students' ideas parallel Steele's; however, they unequivocally realize that "the system," in this case higher education in the form of BMCC, the police, and government, all see them as "under-class blacks" with an initial inclination to do harm, to do crime.

So Brian tries to counter this *class* perspective that lumps *all* people of color in a double bind by beginning with a strong assertion:

African Americans have been striving for a place in society. They have encountered years of bigotry and racial hatred. While dealing with struggle and survival, they've been able to settle in the middle.

It is interesting to note, here, that Brian's entire essay will be based on his notion of "settle," a subtle notion, I might add, that reaches beyond the Steele essay because, in Brian's case, "middle-class" is synonymous with accepting what's being given. Brian's position is a revolutionary one, he believes, and it is that blacks need to reach beyond and move further away from the "under-class," even beyond the "midde class." Brian is adhering to a militancy he's either heard about or experienced: Steele doesn't go far enough. For Brian, this is part of a historical process:

Until the 60s, Afro-Americans didn't have a say in political movements. They just held on to what was handed down to them. During this time Afro-Americans realized the only way to succeed was to take education and freedom.

Along with "settle," now "take," especially as it relates to "education and freedom," provides very interesting insights into Brian's psychology. Brian now feels the need to develop a juxtaposition between Dr. King and Malcolm X to stress the "take" idea, since the two abiding principles of American democracy and self-reliance, "education and freedom," have been categorically kept from the black experience.

But in Brian's commentary, we can see the unfortunate limitations of his knowledge of African American history, a fault, perhaps, of his "schooling":

> Martin Luther King became the first African-American man with powerful influences in the U.S. His encouragement of peaceful rallies and overwhelming speeches made Americans look at what was being done to Afro-Americans. Also he provided Afro-Americans the belief that change can come with hard work. They became more aware of their rights and what abilities they had by being American citizens.

Brian is learning ways of getting his ideas across powerfully. He is using King to bring to the foreground the issue of middle-class values Steele speaks about: "change can come with hard work." In significant ways, Brian's approach parallels Steele's. Steele juxtaposes his personal experiences with contemporary history and politics; similarly, Brian has learned that much can be achieved by using history as a backdrop or as a frame for an argument or discussion.

Brian moves to one of his points, a defense of Steele, and therefore a defense of his own position:

> In Steele's essay, "On Being Black and Middle Class," he said that people outside of his neighborhood treated him, after receiving the experience and the knowledge to make him a writer, differently. "In graduate school I was told by a white professor, 'Well, but . . . you're not really black. I mean, you're not disadvantaged.' In his mind my lack of victim status disqualified me from the race itself." This showed Steele that the country is accepting of him as a writer even if he is black, but that they are not accepting of blacks that are not like him. Steele is like the professor so the professor didn't see black.
>
> In "Do the Right Thing," by Spike Lee, there's a scene in the movie about this. Mookie (Spike) asks the Italian pizza parlor owner's son, Pino, "Who is your favorite rock star?" Pino says, "Prince." Then Mookie asks him, "Who is your favorite comedian?" Pino says, "Eddie Murphy." Mookie points out that they're all black. But Pino responds that, "They're not black." It's the same thing. Some whites think that because certain blacks are accepted by whites as entertainers and athletes and reach a class level they're not black.

This line of argumentation requires action. Malcolm X enters the picture because he represents revolution, the militancy that's essential for Brian's point:

Malcolm X was a con man turned Muslim in his prison time. He was a firm believer of what Dr. King believed intellectually. He believed that the way to solve problems was to attack the problem. Malcolm's strong uplifting message made Afro-Americans believe that there was a way to take a stand in white America's society. Shelby Steele says that, "African Americans achieve middle-class through much hard work and sacrifice." As history shows us Afro-Americans have to struggle just to be in society, so to accept the middle class would just be to recreate the struggle. We can't just settle.

Brian begins and ends his essay with "settle." He uses his understanding of King and Malcolm X to frame what he gleans off Steele's essay to point to the notion that the struggle for acceptance—and identity—in black America is both ongoing and historical. Brian sees his role as historical, as a continuum of struggle: an individual who will not "just settle" for the middle class, a position or identity, he senses, that is also somewhat of a "hand-me-down," though, as Steele suggests, not achievable without hard work and sacrifice.

In Willie, Maricela, and Brian, in fact in everyone I've described so far—Yesenia, Marilynn, and Anna as well—what I am demonstrating is that educational institutions, in their need to immediately "place" and "track," in their zeal to identify, actually retard "remedial" students because of deep abiding biases stemming from our notions of race, class, and gender. Accustomed to this, we act unconsciously, almost by rote. Yet these students want to work, as Brian articulates; they're not afraid to work and they readily accept invigorating challenges. They understand that difficult, hard work is "the way." After all, their lives are difficult and challenging, and demand tremendous intellectual, spiritual, and psychological effort merely to *sobrevivir*.

We place students in "remediation" based on outdated Eurocentric notions of education, which do not even begin to take into account who learners are or how they may perceive themselves and their learning. We see this in Traub's perspective and tone in *City on a Hill*. His frustration and anxiety in the face of overwhelming changes in our culture denotes a lack of imagination, a lack of realization that change is essential to survival.

In *Teaching in America* (1999), speaking about the "pressures of more egalitarian outcomes," Gerald Grant and Christine E. Murray argue that,

> the push that accompanies the second academic revolution is to . . . untrack the schools and to educate all students to higher levels in more inclusive settings. An enormous change in values and beliefs is required to accept the new set of principles that underlies contemporary educational reform. It involves nothing less than a shift from sorting, selecting, and tracking to an emphasis on egalitarianism. No

one argues for equality of outcomes across the board, although re-
ducing the gap in achievement between racial and ethnic groups is
strongly desired. The aim is more inclusive classrooms and cooperative learning that raises the average achievement of all children and
assures that none fall below an acceptable minimum. (224–225)

Grant and Murray's realization that we need "an enormous change
in values and beliefs to accept the new set of principles that underlies
contemporary educational reform" is something some us have known
for quite some time; however, we've been working in isolation, learning
from our students and then changing our own values, trying to affect
"some" institutional changes from within. In higher education, the ancient problem of the isolated nature of the "professor's" existence—the
departmentalization—keeps him or her from embracing and communicating different values and beliefs. Isolation silences change. While I
may have enabled some students, for instance, virtually all of these
same students returned to classrooms that were devoid of any notion of
changes in values and beliefs.

In the past ten years, I can actually name only a handful of professors and teachers who are working progressively to articulate changes
that are "enormous" and that address values and beliefs. This is tragic,
but very real, I think.

The "enormous change in values and beliefs" Grant and Murray
speak about is cultural, societal—and unless this shift begins to occur,
we will inevitably witness a decline in our culture. There is historical
precedence for the moral, spiritual, and intellectual decline of civilizations because they've neglected egalitarian principles meant to level
the socioeconomic environments of all people. We can make the argument that as a society we've been on a decline since the Eisenhower
era, as evidenced by the dissolution of the family, whether because of
divorce, sexual practices, or the need for labor. Labor here is equated
solely to consumerism, or the distortion of individual rights and freedoms for the aggrandizement of profit and production—the commer-
cialization of the individual. The shift in education today is toward highly
skilled and highly specified labor, rather than toward free-thinking,
cultured, and creative individuals who not only understand their own
needs and wants, but who see these self-fulfilling desires as being part
of a larger whole, a part of the needs of society.

Yet, in the remedial students I've presented above, there are signs
of hope—but only if we teachers, administrators, and citizens begin to
fully invest ourselves in learning to read each other so as to give significance to each other's experiences—and see beyond complexion. For
instance, though the writings of these remedial students are not by
any stretch of the imagination "perfect," they do demonstrate a basic
knowledge that enables them to abide by certain rhetorical strategies

that parallel our own. In other words, because these students at the lowest rungs of our educational system, in no-man's-land, do indeed demonstrate or are able to mimic the dominant class's rhetorical strategies, the ground is ripe for inclusive classroom experiences that afford students higher achievement levels.

By initiating all students into college-level work teachers can more fully understand learners and then, by providing these students with a learner-centered environment rich in cooperative learning strategies, we can mutually benefit from this understanding.

To more fully understand this challenge and its implications, my strategy has been to take what I have learned from students at BMCC and extend it to our more mainstream schools. My belief is that what I have done with students at BMCC should likewise provide great benefits to students who have been identified as either "average," "mainstream," or even "above average" and "superior." If the education system is somehow mistaken or misguided at the "remediation" level, the system would be rotten elsewhere.

*   *   *

Knowledge and identity in suburban New Jersey, "an interpretation" fraught with potential, unfolds in the least likely places . . .

> Yet there is
> no return: rolling up out of chaos,
> a nine months' wonder, the city
> the man, an identity—it can't be
> otherwise—an
> interpretation, both ways. Rolling
> up! observe, reverse;
> the drunk the sober; the illustrious
> the gross; one. In ignorance
> a certain knowledge and knowledge,
> undispersed, its own undoing. (William Carlos Williams, *Paterson*)

The William Paterson University of New Jersey, in Wayne, is minutes from the Paterson of William Carlos Williams.

The institution was founded in 1855 as the Paterson City Normal School in response to the growing demand for professional preparation of teachers emerging in the public schools of Paterson. In many ways, the university still carries with it the reputation of being "a school for teachers."

But inner-city blight and ethnic sprawl fleeing New York City, as well as demands from commerce and industry, have indefinitely altered Paterson and its suburbs—and in the interim affected the university. It has been totally remade; there are no discernable remnants from its

Normal School days, except for the School of Education. Now it enrolls more than nine thousand undergraduate and graduate students, supporting twenty-nine undergraduate and seventeen graduate degree programs in five colleges: Arts and Communication, Business, Education, Humanities and Social Sciences, and Science and Health. It has also grown into a 320-acre campus.

The William Paterson University of New Jersey, as is typical of many (sub)urban public institutions, has evolved by necessity, responding to the needs of its immediate community while also trying to lure students from other geographic areas who might be interested in attending a school not quite in New York City, but within range, twenty miles.

I felt like I was light years away, living in an entirely different environment after leaving Borough of Manhattan Community College—so I thought at first blush.

At BMCC *minorities* number 90 percent, closer to even 98 percent of the student population, but at William Paterson University the numbers are a fraction of that, something along the lines of 20 to 23 percent, if that. Which means that students of color usually gather together in small groups, circles in and among the sea of whiteness. Students of color hold to the corners of classrooms, to the margins, metaphors for their identity.

While BMCC can be a metaphor for the *ghettoizing* of experience, the disenfranchizement and alienation we practice in the cause of race and class, William Paterson University is closer to how we live openly and collectively, on the surface and within groups we're comfortable with—the suburbanization of experience: life experienced in labyrinthine strip malls, in cars, on labyrinthine roadways and highways, and then in more malls, large ones with amusement rides.

The so-called "white" students at the university are, for the most part, first generation and primarily Catholic Italian Americans—translation: well-behaved, non–risk takers, silent, and eager to do what they are told. They keep to the schedule, turn assignments in on time, follow orders. They like sitting in rows and keeping quiet; only a few, three at most, usually respond to an open-ended question in a class. The remainder wait passively in silence.

A colleague once depressingly remarked to me that, "Our mission is to turn out 'perfect' mid-level managers to fit into the economic system. Not intellectuals." That's it. Plain and simple.

When I first came to the university yet another colleague said something to me that was all-too-often repeated by others, even at departmental meetings: "Our students care about their cars first, their jobs second, and then school. School is merely a means to an end, a better job." Case closed.

The same notion I'd heard at BMCC also permeated this university: there's not much one can do with these students; the occasional "stars" do exist, so one teaches to them. But the majority, well, mediocrity is the aspiration.

My first impression of the school was that the noise, the ruckus, the liveliness, and the energy of BMCC was gone or, as I learned, was well hidden, one might say even repressed. (In keeping with this decorum, Paterson students can register for classes "online," while the BMCC students stand on endless lines, on-a-line, as I've described earlier.)

After a semester of succumbing to the deafening silence in my classrooms, I decided to attack the problem by revising one of the most staid courses on the books, the Introduction to Literature course.

In "Authority, Collaboration and Ownership: Sources for Critical Writing and Portfolio Assessment" (Vila 1999) I suggest that the Introduction to Literature course is no more than the bastard child of most English Departments. With this course, we are saying to students that they have indeed achieved some level of proficiency, usually in composition, but they don't have the sophistication, nor the "proper" intellectual foundation to really understand "our" Literature. And adding insult to injury, we assign expensive, giant tomes, Introduction to Literature texts, which are more appropriate to weight-lifting classes than to any study of literature. Aggravating the problem even further is the number of students taking these classes, usually above thirty, so we don't assign writing, or the writing we do assign is minimal.[3]

What in fact do we accomplish in these classes, especially since we also relegate the teaching of Introduction to Literature courses to either graduate students or adjuncts, though we consider the course to be a portal to the English major? After English Composition, the Introduction to Literature course is usually a student's "first look" at the study of literature and all this entails, so how do we indeed "advertise" and promote our profession to undergraduates?

I found that I couldn't answer my own questions—or maybe I didn't quite like what I was thinking.

So I revised the course to parallel the writing courses I've described earlier, selecting literature that might respond to the problems I was noting in my classes: silence, lack of motivation, little to no enthusiasm—the "tell me what to do" syndrome. I chose less literature, too, so that we could delve deeply into something—an inquiry into our relationships with texts, communities, and ourselves that would entail varieties of writing.[4]

If students are to take literature, then they too should have the luxury of sitting in the writer's seat, I thought. Do we not ask students to think as mathematicians, in fact to be mathematicians in math classes? Sociologists in sociology courses? Historians in history courses? Why not writers in literature courses?

Each student in the course was required to keep a journal, a free space for reflecting, brainstorming, thinking. During each class there was writing, conversation, questions and answers, group work. Students were compelled to share thoughts. I wanted students to come into each class with the anticipation of a performance. They did, and this made all the difference in the world. The binds of conformity and complacency were broken, at least for this class—and students reached well beyond mediocrity, an achievement demonstrated by their end-of-term writing portfolios.

I also assigned a term paper in the course, a paper that grew like a flowering plant from our earliest readings and discussions. Approaching the course as primarily a writing course in which literature would be both model and stimuli suggests certain possibilities: the construction of a learning environment that enables students to understand—to realize—the relationships between the many varieties (genres) of writing they create and themselves; the integral relationship between reading and writing, aesthetics and authorship; the understanding that writing grows, changes, evolves, and is a profoundly human creation.

With little urging from me, students discovered that the seed for their term papers was sown on the first day of class and that the writing truly belonged to them. This approach virtually guarantees student commitment to projects. Issues concerning plagiarism are nearly nonexistent since their work evolves slowly from the beginning of the term. Most important, it is personal. We share this ongoing work throughout the term so that it must be attended to over many weeks and through many in-class workshops.

On the first day of class, without as much as an introduction, or without "running" through the syllabus, I asked students to take a few moments to write about "friendship." I gave them about five to seven minutes. Then I asked them to write about "passion." Following "passion," it was "love," and after "love," "relationships."

We spent the remainder of the class sharing our thoughts. At first students raised their hands, hesitantly, as they had done in Yesenia's class. Then, after they began speaking, more students jumped in without raising their hands. And eventually they began speaking to one another across the room. I let the energy go. At moments, some students looked at me, nervously, I believe, because I simply stayed off to one side and let them speak to one another for long periods and thus carry the flow, the energy, and the direction. They weren't accustomed to seeing a teacher *not* control the dynamics of a classroom. I let them take this initial control of the class so that we could have an understanding for the duration of the course: the learning is yours, the student's, it's about you—I'm merely a guide so you need to take control *from* me.

Then I stopped it, suddenly.

They looked at me, startled.

"What just happened?" I asked. "Stop a minute and think about what you thought about the course when you first came in, then think about your thoughts when I gave you the prompts, "friendship," "love," and so on . . . What went through your minds as you wrote? What did you think you were involved in? Think about how we started sharing and where we are now: What happened? Where are we? What are we doing?"

"It's different," said a student.

"Well, we got to know what each of us was thinking," said another. "That was good."

"I don't know. I think it's different too. We got right into it instead of the teacher doing all the talking," recorded another student.

My point is twofold: to demystify Literature into literature and to dispel the tension and anxiety in the room. I also want to model "the work" for the semester: writing, sharing, and reflecting, then writing again. In this manner, writing is not a chore, or even a discipline, but rather an integral way of investigating ideas, questions, unknowns.

I then pass out a couple of sonnets by Shakespeare.

"I'll read them, then you tell me what you see," I say.

As has always been the case, students see in the poetry what they've written about earlier and what they have been communicating to each other. They speak out without my asking for volunteers.

The most poignant comment came from a young woman: "Wow, I thought I was so modern, but I can see from these poems that our ways of thinking about love and passion are quite old."

She was reacting to Sonnet 29:

> When, in disgrace with fortune and men's eyes,
> I all alone beweep my outcast state,
> And trouble deaf heaven with my bootless cries,
> And look upon myself and curse my fate,
> Wishing me like to one more rich in hope,
> Featur'd like him, like him with friends possess'd,
> Desiring this man's art and that man's scope,
> With what I most enjoy contended least;
> Yet in these thoughts myself almost despising,
> Haply I think on thee, and then my state,
> Like to the lark at break of day arising
> From sullen earth, sings hymns at heaven's gate;
>   For thy sweet love rememb'red such wealth brings
>   That then I scorn to change my state with kings.

What we are seeing here is that precondition to all appreciation of literature: connection between student and poem, student and text.

In every succeeding class throughout the semester, students begin by warming up: they do 5 to 10 minutes of freewriting. They use this time to acclimate to the notion of being writers and of being in the company of literature: we're going to read literature, study it, describe it, explain it, and write about it and in response to it. I use the freewriting time at the beginning of each class—no more than ten minutes—to enable students to leave their former, physical world of "other" courses and activities outside before they enter into the sanctum of literature.

On January 26, 1996, while we're very much still working with poetry, one of my most ambitious students, Kevin, writes in his journal:

> When I saw her it felt like lightning striking me. I did not know what to say or what to do. Every time I saw her my heart leaped. I wanted to let her know, but I could not tell her. I instead made her laugh, at every chance I got I walked her home sometimes. I gave her presents for her birthday. I gave her cards. I finally told her. She did not care. She told me she liked my friend and asked me to talk to him. Being so in love I only wanted her happiness and so I became their intermediary.

It is one of Kevin's earliest attempts to put feeling into words, to approximate the poetry that he is reading. Kevin had never before written poetry, he told us, but he finally shares his first attempt with us about a third of the way through the course. Kevin's poem, which he read aloud to the class, is called, "Our Poem,"

> One more time around,
> The silicone chip inside her head turns to overdrive,
> I saw the sign.
> What's the matter with me.
> Love you, Hate you, Live or Die.
> Roads are winding, Lights are blinding.
> Save Me, I'm willing to give it another try.
> You said you would never leave me.
> I love you so much, I'll drive you crazy too.
> I don't owe you anything but I will never be free.
> Despite all my rage, I'm still just a rat in a cage
> Nothing's wrong, it's all right. Stop laying blame.
> I did nothing wrong. Don't turn away from me,
> I need someone to hold on to.
> My pain is self-chosen. Breathe In, Breathe Out, Breathe
> Out. This is the end of innocence.
> Escape is never the safest plan.

For someone so young, romantic, and impressionable, and for someone who admitted to not having read much poetry, not a bad first time, I think. However, for our purposes, it's relevant to note how Kevin's readings of the poetry, following our early prompts, actually bring forth certain feelings, thoughts, and emotions that have been lurking in him for quite some time. The point is that the learning environment is stimulating enough, and safe enough, to enable Kevin to begin to dwell on something he needs to gain some perspective on to go forth. He is reaching toward one of my major goals: trying on the "shoes," if you will, of the poet, whether they've done so in the past or not. Some giggle at Kevin's poem and at their own early clumsy attempts. Others welcome this opportunity since they confess to writing some form or another of verse in "private places."

Literature and writing are perfect vehicles for this kind of exploration, instruments for self-awareness and expression: they are experienced as tools, then, not obstacles or demands created by an institution. Literature is experienced for what it is, life blood. And in the interim, I'm learning something about what the student sees, what he's experiencing, and where he may be going.

Kevin, like all the students in the course, is keeping a weekly journal that allows for the discovery of ideas and the development of a reading-writing relationship. My role in response to the students' journals is to motivate, to point and comment positively, to push gently, to nudge carefully—and to demonstrate my genuine interest in what students are saying by commenting in ways that encourage the associations we are all making between our own lives, our writing, and the literature we're experiencing, alone and in the group. I comment on word choice and compliment them on their thinking, which I often find quite invigorating. "Keep this in mind as it could be useful later for more formal writing," I write in response to a particularly keen observation.

I routinely ask students to reflect on what they've been thinking, feeling, or noticing, either about the course, the content, or the way things are going in the class itself during our day-to-day activities.[5]

One of the students writes:

> Love is complicated. The Greeks had 3 different terms for love and we must understand this subject. He said that there were plenty of people who did the same things I did to let that special someone know how I feel. I wonder how they fared? Education is complicated too: we see institutions as knowledge but lack the passion that goes with getting this knowledge. Nothing is just pure emotion anymore. There is only blind need to acquire information. This is not because we love it but because we are told to.

I found this reflection quite surprising. The student writes about "education" and asserts that there is some relationship between "emotion" and the attainment of knowledge. I had no idea that this student was thinking about these things. I greatly appreciate being let into the world of my students, the perceptions they have that are based on influences—institutions—and perhaps the subsequent behavior that is aggravated by these conditions—"blind need."

The student's final line, which places the individual in the role of some sort of "machine," or a person who is not a "free-thinker," is alarming: "This is not because we love it but because we are told to." It says volumes about how energetic and imaginative we have to be in challenging our students' sense of the status quo. These journals are a window into the minds of students at work making a personal meaning out of literature and writing.

In the short story section of the course, students were exposed to a variety of themes and styles: "What We Talk About When We Talk About Love," "The Lottery," "A Rose for Emily," "Patriotism," and "A Good Man is Hard to Find." I wanted to create a course where students could begin to make connections between their own perspectives on life, the reading materials, and the writing; and I wanted to do this by using writing as the vehicle to find our voices.

Many of the students understood that they were working on expanding the ideas they uncovered and shared from the first day of class. They began making formal and informal connections in their readings and their writings, slowly accruing the ideas, the materials, the skills, and the incentives to engage in the study of literature. Experienced like this, Introduction to Literature is not *just another course*, but a unique way to examine the conditions of history, our experiences and, perhaps, our future.

It is important to note that there is little difference between the students at William Paterson University who had already completed Freshman Composition and the more advanced Introduction to Literature, and my former students in remediation at BMCC. Yes, it does take the BMCC remedial student longer to produce comparable material. Yes, the BMCC student may be less comfortable with reading and writing about literature. However, the Paterson students are by no means "great" or accomplished in their abilities. On the contrary, their work is mediocre, it's "okay." Mediocrity is, however, the "norm" in many (sub)urban colleges and universities where the population is diverse, and complicated by the school's need to expand, enlarge, or offer more to more based on the administration's perception of the community's needs weighed against the marketplace. Administrators justify anything with this pronouncement, though little analysis and criticism have taken place to determine what is actually worthwhile and beneficial to the learning community. Arguably, the notion of "community," when coupled to blind "growth" of this nature, is lost completely.

It's also not difficult to see why a teacher might interpret this environment as merely an assembly line for middle-management types. However, we can give some semblance of hope to these students by offering material in a way that challenges staid notions of education. Higher education need not merely be a means to an end, a job. Higher education can be—in fact needs to be—an experience where students and teachers become partners in a lifelong process of inquiry, learning, conversing and sharing, with the "end" of advancing society. We can deal with our differences, but only if we make the classroom a place for experimentation, where we test what we know by placing ourselves in rigorous circumstances by using challenging materials.

I want to close this chapter—and this book—by illustrating one student's progression through the semester. Kevin, the young man I mentioned earlier, is a black student who first sat at the back of the room, but who ended up pursuing me well into the following two semesters with questions about literature, writing, and the "profession." Kevin's peculiar genius is that he finds ways to bring the writing and literature together into his life. Writing, communicating, reading literature—all are instruments for Kevin's articulation of the strongly held convictions and ideas he's obviously been contemplating for quite some time.

It's not surprising that Kevin's first "formal" essay is titled "The Desire For Acceptance and Love" because this is a theme that occupies him for much of the semester:

> Two things people can desire are Acceptance and Love. Desire is a craving need that must be satisfied. Desires, unfortunately, can lead to gratification or heart break. These desires can lead to stability, security or happiness if properly invested. People's desires can lead to friendship, companionship, or even love. Whatever the object or thing, everyone desires something. The hunt to quench this need has many perils. One can never tell what another person is feeling or thinking. The venturing out can be dangerous to the heart because one can have their hopes smashed to the ground. The choice of the other person seems to be like a game of chance.

Much of what Kevin writes about throughout the course—his own poetry, the criticisms of poems and stories, the freewritings, and the reflections—is in this first paragraph. We can see where his more formalized ideas come from. He's able to evolve an authoritative tone because he has been working through these ideas from different perspectives, forms, and voices since the first day of class.

> People can desire a type of stability by acceptance. Mostly at the high school level, students need to be accepted by their peers. This acceptance can give confidence and a sense of security in that there will always be someone there to comfort you whenever you may need it. There will always be someone who will believe in you and not betray you. There is a type of comfort while in the midst of one's friends. There is security in knowing that if the world gets too much to handle, thee will be someone there to run to. This friend may be able to take your mind off of your troubles. Friendship is very important to the individual.

In this second paragraph, Kevin breaks new ground, the daunting world of high school and the need to belong; however, it's also refreshing to note his sensibilities. Kevin is describing who he is and what he values. As a teacher, this affects my approach to this student because I'm gaining insights into his psychology as well as his value system. It helps me to communicate with him more effectively.

Kevin ultimately gets to his ideas on love. Here again he's speaking from experience:

> The down side to love occurs when the feeling is not shared. The feeling that follows is not passion but of pain and hurt. The pain of being shot down is not one anyone desires. This is why Love is a game of chance. Once can never tell if the other person feels the same. All the emotion and lust seems to be wasted. After the immediate hurt there comes the regret. One regrets telling the other person or even having felt that way in the first place. After the regret comes the anger. One feels angry that all your time and heart felt sentiment goes to waste. Then comes a last feeling of hope in which you still think that there is a chance, even though your mind is telling you to move on. From the time the other person refuses the advancement, the logical mind tries to regain control to make things better. It will take a long time before you will try to love again.

Kevin concludes his essay saying that, "We must keep striving on until we find the people we can be most comfortable with. The others we meet are just road signs to Acceptance and Love."

It is instructive, at this juncture, to look once again at Kevin's final portfolio letter as he continues his self-assessment:

> The course, though very rigorous, was enjoyable. I was able to connect most of the stories, and their recurring themes to help me formulate my thesis and my final essay. The approach to work has improved my writing skills even more than when I first arrived. Especially enjoyable was the use of the journal. Putting feelings and thoughts on paper has always been very difficult for me. Eventually I got used to the idea and I think I can do it a little better.
>
> I have come a long way from my first day of class. I was standing outside the door, wondering whether to come in or not (late as usual) and then you said that all late papers will have points taken off for every day it was late and this included weekends. It was then that I decided to leave as quickly as I could so as to not get caught by a madman. Funny how first impressions can be completely wrong.

Something compelled Kevin to stay. There was a relationship between content and context on that first day that spoke to him and challenged him. Of the many things that Kevin perhaps learned in the course, this last paragraph is significant. Not only did he work through his "status quo," mediocrity, but he's also learned that he can attain more simply by working intelligently, creatively, and intensely. He's learned to contextualize material to suit his ongoing inquiry into the self.

Kevin is realizing that his learning is a journey and this lesson, I would argue, is helped along by the structure of the course: the premise that learning is lifelong, that literature and writing are partners in this exciting endeavor, and that much of learning, as Socrates says, involves remembering.

Truth is process; it's searching, inquiring, and laboring, all with great effort and verve, to examine the interrelatedness that exists between one's experiences and the rest of the world.

In his final portfolio letter, Kevin writes:

> When I took English 110, I learned some basic steps on how to write a composition and made some improvements in the construction of my sentences. Sentence structure was emphasized because without good sentences, it is impossible to have a good paragraph and these two components are essential in writing. I thought that a good and well structured composition was enough to fulfill the requirements of a good piece of writing. However, writing takes much more than just that. When I write, many other things are to be taken into consideration such as the transition from one point to another, sticking to the main topic, illustrate and use sources, whatever it might be completely, and other little things that make writing interesting and accurate . . .
>
> A journal is essential in any humanities course, but for this particular one, I do not think it would be possible to run a course like this without journals. By keeping a journal, further assignments are accomplished much easier, as in the case of our term paper, and it is the best source for storing ideas from the readings. Through the journal, I could compare myself to the characters in the readings and it also gave me the opportunity to talk about my journal experiences and feelings which was a great therapy for me.

A classmate of Kevin's, Yudelnia, had a similar experience. The course served as a vehicle to learn how to learn, to understand the context of the need to learn, and ultimately, as Yudelnia says in her letter, to be "better prepared for a more productive life and ready to put into practice everything I learned."

We can turn to Emerson one last time.

> There is one mind common to all individual men. Every man is an inlet to the same and to all of the same. He that is once admitted to the right of reason is made a freeman of the whole estate. What Plato has thought, he may think; what a saint has felt, he may feel; what at any time has befallen any man, he can understand. Who hath access to this universal mind is a party to all that is or can be done, for this is the only sovereign agent. (1960, 7)

This is Emerson paraphrasing what Socrates says to Crito. We can all access what Plato has thought—we already know it—though we may go about achieving this access in different ways or forms. What we require as learners is an environment in which our *life-affirming acts* can be synthesized by a process, which we define ourselves, with the outside world, the world of objects and challenging ideas, the world of differences. This is indeed my most potent guide when I approach a learning situation: that we're interrelated in basic and important ways, and that what I know, you also know: it's all in the asking and in the questioning, the manner or process by which we engage in learning.

I believed that Yesenia could see, could work, could create if she had a meaningful context. I believed, firmly, that others at BMCC could do the same—and they did. These students proved to me that they are capable and willing to engage in rich, wonderful relationships with texts, with each other, and with the teacher, if—and only if—they are included in the conversation.

After leaving BMCC, and while also experiencing the educational trials and tribulations of my own children, I have found that for the most part, we pay more attention to the institution—to dogma or empty rhetoric—than to the student. For the most part, the status quo dominates, profoundly so, even in some very insightful discussions about education reform. Thus reform does not happen. In all, what I find missing is "the story," the narratives that we interweave and use to re-create ourselves and our curricula. After all, we teachers own it—or should.

Now, as the dominance of information technology makes itself felt, there is an even greater reason to centralize our students in their learning environments, and to make their learning even more intimate, and then begin to articulate the narrative of the "universal mind" so that we, too, can be "party to all that is or can be done."

We must reach out to the Yesenias, the Kevins, the Yudelnias of our world, by committing our entire selves to the classroom, and therefore ourselves.

We need life-affirming acts. And these begin by uttering our stories, first and foremost.

Notes

1. In a class of 25 remedial writers, I routinely examine six journals weekly. My intention is to dialogue with students through their journal entries. I do not comment on grammar. I comment solely on content. The criteria for the journal is that they'll be rewarded according to how much they write. So if a student fails the WAT, and it's a borderline failure, a score of "6," say, instead of the passing "8," then a 'good' journal will get them over the hump, provided they have done well in the rest of the course.

2. W. B. Yeats, "Among School Children," in *The Norton Anthology of Modern Poetry*, Richard Ellmann and Robert O'Clair, eds. (New York: W.W. Norton, 1973). Stanza vi reads:

Plato thought nature but a spume that plays
Upon a ghostly paradigm of things;
Solider Aristotle played the taws
Upon the bottom of a king of kings;
World-famous golden-thighed Pythagoras
Fingered upon a fiddle-stick or strings
What a star sang and careless Muses heard:
Old clothes upon old sticks to scare a bird.

Interestingly, on March 14, 1926, in his notebook, Yeats writes, "Topic for poem—School children and the thought that life will waste them perhaps that no possible life can fulfill our dreams or even their teacher's hope. Bring in the old thought that life prepares for what never happens."

3. On either side of the socioeconomic-educational spectrum there are similarities with the remedial world: little writing is expected of students; what is assigned, though, is usually characteristic of an "end" piece, a summary, or a way to bring work to a close—nothing else. Writing is not used to investigate or to evolve an inquiry, and there's no writing for self-discovery.

4. One colleague read my approach as "avant-garde" and "leftist," a liberal approach, she said, that did not concentrate on a "breath of knowledge" students need and that requires "close reading," she continued, in order to get through the long list of "works." Another colleague, one that actually observed my class, took another tack: she criticized me for giving students work that was beyond their capabilities, in this case, Margaret Atwood's *The Handmaid's Tale.*

5. By "routinely" I mean at different times during a given day. Usually I may have a planned Reflection, like when I know that we will be involved in something particularly refreshing, as I've shown above when we met for the first time; other times, it's a matter of realizing when the class has moved into particularly provocative areas of understanding, so I sense that it may prove useful to think about the learning that's going on, the pedagogy, enabling students to witness themselves in the act of learning. This requires keen observation and a *feel* for the class's energies. In turn, these reflections enforce the notion of taking responsibility for one's learning.

References

Adam, Barry D. 1978. *The Survival of Domination*. New York & Oxford: Elsevier.

Barthes, Roland. 1977. *Image Music Text*. Stephen Heath, trans. New York: Hill and Wang.

Birkerts, Sven. 1994. *The Gutenberg Elegies*. New York: Fawcett Columbine.

Bloom, Harold. 1973. *The Anxiety of Influence*. London, Oxford, New York: Oxford University Press.

Borges, Jorge Luis. 1975. "La Noche de Los Dones." *El Libro de Arena*. Buenos Aires, Argentina: Ultramar-Emercé.

Brookfield, Stephen D. 1990. *The Skillful Teacher*. San Francisco and Oxford: Jossey-Bass.

Calkins, Lucy. 1994. *The Art of Teaching Writing*. Portsmouth, NH: Heinemann.

Capra, Fritjof. 1988. *The Turning Point*. New York: Bantam Doubleday.

Derrida, Jacques. 1976. *Of Grammatology*. Trans. Gayatri Chakravorty Spivak. Baltimore, MD: Hopkins University Press.

———. 1981. *The Philosophy of John Dewey*. John J. McDermott, ed. Chicago and London: University of Chicago Press.

Dewey, John. 1938. *Experience and Education*. New York and London: Collier Books.

Eco, Umberto. 1984. *The Role of the Reader*. Bloomington, IN: Indiana University Press.

Elbow, Peter. 1981. *Writing with Power*. New York and Oxford: Oxford University Press.

Emerson, Ralph Waldo. 1960. *Selections from Ralph Waldo*. Stephen E. Whicher, ed. Boston, MA: Houghton Mifflin.

———. 1990. *Emerson, Essays: First and Second Series*. New York: First Vintage Books/Library of America Edition.

Foucault, Michel. 1979. *Discipline & Punish*. New York: Vintage Books.

Freire, Paulo. 1972. *Pedagogy of the Oppressed*. New York: Herder and Herder.

Friedman, Thomas L. 1999. "A Manifesto for the Fast World." *New York Times Magazine*, 28 March, 43.

Fulwiler, Toby, ed. 1987. *The Journal Book*. Portsmouth, NH: Boynton/Cook Publishers.

Gardner, Howard. 1993. *Frames of Mind*. New York: Basic Books.

Ginsberg, Allen. 1985. "Ode to Failure." In *Contemporary American Poetry*, 4th ed. A. Poulin Jr. Boston, MA: Houghton Mifflin.

Gramsci, Antonio. 1988. *An Antonio Gramsci Reader*. David Forgas, ed. New York: Schocken Books.

Grant, Gerald, and Christine E. Murray. 1999. *Teaching in America*. Cambridge, MA and London: Harvard University Press.

Hawisher, Gail E., and Cynthia L. Selfe. 1997. "Wedding the Technologies of Writing Portfolios and Computers." In *Situating Portfolios, Four Perspectives*, ed. Kathleen Blake Yancey and Irwin Weiser. Logan, UT: Utah State University Press.

Kozol, Jonathan. 1991. *Savage Inequalities*. New York: Crown.

———. 1995. *Amazing Grace*. New York: Crown.

Lanham, Richard, A. 1993. *The Electronic World, Democracy, Technology and the Arts*. Chicago and London: University of Chicago Press.

McCormick, Kathleen. 1994. *The Culture of Reading & the Teaching of English*. Manchester, England, and New York: Manchester University Press.

McLaren, Peter. 1989. *Life in Schools*. New York and London: Longman.

Merleau-Ponty, M. 1994. *Phenomenology of Perception*. London: Routledge.

Noyes, Russell. 1956. *English Romantic Poetry and Prose*. New York and London: Oxford University Press.

Ong, Walter. 1982. *Orality and Literacy*. London and New York: Metheun & Co.

Park, Emily. 1998. "Kurt Vonnegut Lectures to Sold-Out Audience." *Colgate Maroon News*, vol. CXXII, no. 16 (13 February).

Postrel, Virginia. 1998. *The Future and Its Enemies*. New York: Free Press.

Powell, Walter W., and Elisabeth S. Clemens. 1998. *Private Action and the Public Good*. New Haven and London: Yale University Press.

Rodriguez, Abraham Jr. 1992. *The Boy Without a Flag*. Minneapolis, MN: Milkweed.

Rodriguez, Richard. 1982. *Hunger of Memory*. Boston, MA: David R. Godine.

Rose, Mike. 1989. *Lives on the Boundary*. New York: Penguin Books.

Sandholtz, Judith Haymore, Cathy Ringstaff, and David C. Dwyer. 1997. *Teaching with Technology: Creating Student-Centered Classrooms*. New York: Teachers College Press.

Sizer, Theodore R. 1996. *Horace's Hope*. Boston and New York: Houghton Mifflin.

Steele, Shelby. 1995. "On Being Black and Middle Class." *The Best American Essays, College Edition*, ed. Robert Atwan. Boston, MA: Houghton Mifflin.

Summerfield, Judith, and Geoffrey Summerfield. 1986. *Texts & Contexts*. New York: Random House.

Traub, James. 1994a. *City on a Hill*. Reading, MA; Menlo Park, CA; New York: Addison-Wesley.

———. 1994b. "Class Struggle." *The New Yorker.* 19 September, 1994.

———. 1999. "Stuck in Bilingual Education." *New York Times Magazine.* 31 January, sec. 6.

Vila, Hector J. 1999. "Authority, Collaboration and Ownership: Sources for Critical Writing and Porfolio Assessment." In *Teaching in the 21st Century: Adapting Writing Pedagogies to the College Curriculum,* ed. Barbara Smith. New York: Garland Press.

Villanueva, Jr., Victor. 1993. *Bootstraps.* Urbana, IL: National Council of Teachers of English.

Vinz, Ruth. 1996. *Composing a Teaching Life.* Portsmouth, NH: Boynton/Cook.

Warmington, Eric H., and Philip G. Rouse. 1956. *Great Dialogues of Plato.* Trans. W. H. D. Rouse. New York and Scarborough, Ontario: New American Library.

West, Cornel. 1993. *Prophetic Thought in Postmodern Times.* Monroe, ME: Common Courage Press.

———. 1994. *Race Matters.* New York: Vintage Books.

Williams, William Carlos. 1958. *Paterson.* New York: New Directions.

Zinsser, William. 1990. *On Writing Well,* 4th ed. New York: Harper Perennial.

Index